CAMPAIGN 341

THE LONG MARCH 1934–35

The rise of Mao and the beginning of modern China

BENJAMIN LAI

ILLUSTRATED BY ADAM HOOK
Series editor Marcus Cowper

OSPREY PUBLISHING
Bloomsbury Publishing Plc
PO Box 883, Oxford, OX1 9PL, UK
1385 Broadway, 5th Floor, New York, NY 10018, USA
E-mail: info@ospreypublishing.com
www.ospreypublishing.com

OSPREY is a trademark of Osprey Publishing Ltd

First published in Great Britain in 2019

A catalogue record for this book is available from the British Library.

ISBN: PB: 978 1 4728 3401 0
          ePub: 978 1 4728 3402 7
          ePDF: 978 1 4728 3400 3
          XML: 978 1 4728 3403 4

19 20 21 22 23   10 9 8 7 6 5 4 3 2 1

Index by Nick Hayhurst
Typeset in Myriad Pro and Sabon
Maps by Bounford.com
3D BEVs by The Black Spot
Page layouts by PDQ Digital Media Solutions, Bungay, UK
Printed and bound by Bell & Bain Ltd., Glasgow G46 7UQ

Artist's note

Readers may care to note that the original paintings from which the colour
plates in this book were prepared are available for private sale. All
reproduction copyright whatsoever is retained by the Publishers. The artist
can be contacted at the following address:

Scorpio Gallery, Mill Farm House, 158 Mill Road, Hailsham, East Sussex BN27
2SH, UK

The Publishers regret that they can enter into no correspondence upon
this matter.

Osprey Publishing supports the Woodland Trust, the UK's leading woodland
conservation charity.

To find out more about our authors and books visit
www.ospreypublishing.com. Here you will find extracts, author
interviews, details of forthcoming events and the option to sign up for
our newsletter.

Dedication

To all who are facing difficulties in life: Be inspired by the spirit of the Long
March. Despite some very difficult roads ahead, march on; it will eventually
lead you to your promised land. Fight on, have faith and never give up.

Author's note

Throughout this book, I have used the Pinyin system, the current UN
standard for modern Chinese transliteration. The only exception to the rule
is for some key personalities where the Wade–Giles/Yale romanized forms
are better known: for example, Chiang Kaishek (instead of Jiang Jieshi),
Kuomintang (instead of Guomindang), etc. In writing Chinese names, I
follow the Asian naming system where family name precedes the given
name. A list of Chinese names is provided at the end of this work as
an appendix.
A list of Chinese place names mentioned in this work is also included in the
Appendix. In the 80-plus years since the Long March, many of the names of
these locations have changed. However, in order for the modern reader to
follow the events more easily, I have chosen modern geographical names
over old names, although for reference purposes I have included former
names in brackets in the Appendix.

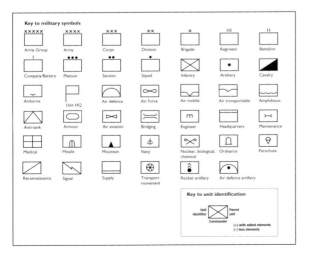

CONTENTS

China prior to October 1934

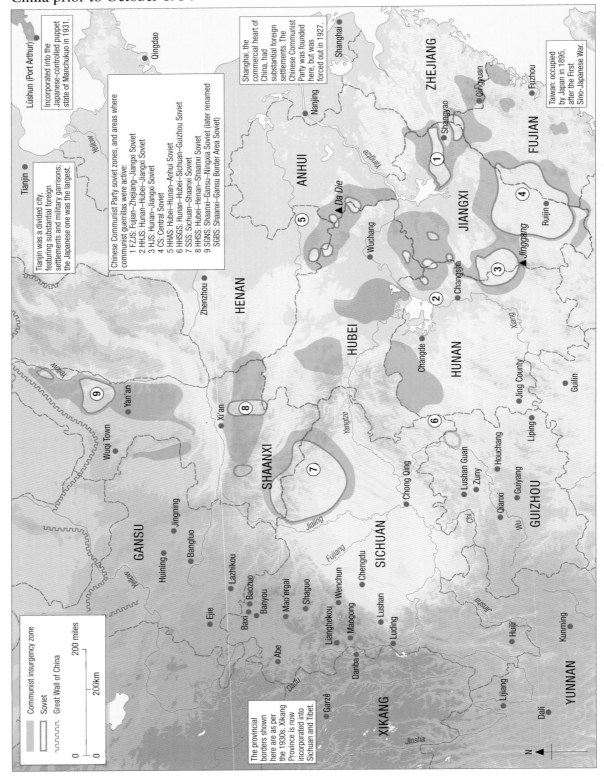

Lüshun (Port Arthur)

Incorporated into the Japanese-controlled puppet state of Manchukuo in 1931.

Tianjin was a divided city, featuring substantial foreign settlements and military garrisons; the Japanese one was the largest.

Chinese Communist Party soviet zones, and areas where communist guerrillas were active:
1 FZJS: Fujian–Zhejiang–Jiangxi Soviet
2 HHJS: Hunan–Hubei–Jiangxi Soviet
3 HJS: Hunan–Jiangxi Soviet
4 CS: Central Soviet
5 HHAS: Hubei–Hunan–Anhui Soviet
6 HHSGS: Hunan–Hubei–Sichuan–Guizhou Soviet
7 SSS: Sichuan–Shaanxi Soviet
8 HHSS: Hubei–Henan–Shaanxi Soviet
9 SGNS: Shaanxi–Gansu–Ningxia Soviet (later renamed SGBS: Shaanxi–Gansu Border Area Soviet)

Shanghai: the commercial heart of China, had substantial foreign settlements. The Chinese Communist Party was founded here, but was forced out in 1927.

Taiwan: occupied by Japan in 1895, after the First Sino-Japanese War.

The provincial borders shown here are as per the 1930s. Xikang Province is now incorporated into Sichuan and Tibet.

Communist insurgency zone
Soviet
Great Wall of China

0   200km
0   200 miles

N

Provinces: ZHEJIANG, ANHUI, JIANGXI, FUJIAN, HENAN, HUBEI, HUNAN, SHAANXI, GANSU, SICHUAN, GUIZHOU, XIKANG, YUNNAN

Cities/places: Qingdao, Tianjin, Qingyuan, Fuzhou, Shanghai, Nanjing, Shangyao, Rujin, Jinggang, Da Die, Wuchang, Changsha, Changde, Zhenzhou, Jing County, Guilin, Xi'an, Yan'an, Wuqi Town, Liping, Houchang, Guiyang, Jingning, Bangluo, Huining, Lazhikou, Chong Qing, Lushan Guan, Zuny, Qianxi, Wu, Ejie, Baxi, Baozuo, Banyou, Mao'ergai, Shaguo, Lianghekou, Wenchun, Chengdu, Lushan, Luding, Huili, Kunming, Abe, Danba, Garzê, Lijiang, Dali

Rivers: Yellow, Yangtze, Xiang, Jialing, Fujiang, Dadu, Jinsha, Chi

ORIGINS OF THE CAMPAIGN

The Long March of the Red Army was the trial by fire of the Chinese Communist Party (CCP), and 'the greatest strategic retreat in military history', according to the eminent Harvard sinologist Roderick MacFarquhar. Shortly after Chiang Kaishek became the leader of the Kuomintang (KMT – the Chinese Nationalist Party) in 1926, the Communists had to withdraw into the countryside to continue their struggle. In 1934, the Communist leader Mao Zedong's rural stronghold in Ruijin was surrounded by Nationalist troops, and they made a bold escape move, setting out on an epic quest for survival that lasted just over a year. The Central (First) Red Army, numbering in the tens of thousands, marched across half of China, passing over 18 mountain ranges and 24 rivers, before meeting up with other Communist armies and establishing their famous base at Yan'an, from where they would continue their revolution. The Long March established Mao as the absolute leader of the CCP and inspired many people to follow the red banner.

Although the Long March was a military disaster for the Chinese Communists, from its ashes arose a political triumph that eventually led to the foundation of modern China. The events changed Mao Zedong from just another ambitious leader into the head of the CCP and later chairman of the most populous nation in the world.

THE STRATEGIC SITUATION

The Xinhai Revolution of 1911 oversaw the end of 4,000 years of imperial rule in China and the establishment of a republic known to the world as the Republic of China (ROC). The spark which led to the overthrow of the imperial system was struck in Wuchang, the capital of Hubei Province in central China. A group of discontented soldiers within the Wuchang garrison rebelled against the much-resented Manchu people, which created a ripple effect that led to a tidal wave of copycat rebellions that eventually saw the collapse of the Manchu-led imperial government. However, the young republic did not have an easy start. The country was in chaos and was besieged by countless rebellions and counter-rebellions. Murders and assassinations were common, as each faction fought to ensure leadership over this new republic. In the first decade of its life, the ROC was to see a number of politicians enter and exit the revolving doors of power, while it was simultaneously besieged by multiple groups and political factions each claiming to represent the true state.

OPPOSITE
China in the early 1930s was far from united. Aside from Japanese aggression and CCP rebellion, Chiang Kaishek's control was only effective in the northern coastal region, the lower reaches of the Yangtze and in Zhejiang Province. Hunan, Guizhou, Yunnan, part of Anhui, Henan, Gansu and Shaanxi provinces were under the control of warlord generals.

In the second decade of the 20th century, Marxist ideas were beginning to take root in China, especially among intellectuals and students. They saw its revolutionary concepts as a means of saving and reviving the nation. One such group of young men, led by Li Dazhao (the chief librarian at Peking University) and Chen Duxiu, decided to create a new political party – the CCP – in 1921, after receiving assistance and encouragement from the Communist International (COMINTERN) agent Grigori Voitinsky. A mere 12 men took part in this historic first meeting of the CCP, including Mao Zedong (an assistant to Li at the library), and a radical Peking University student called Zhang Guotao. Both men were to later fall out, each taking different paths.

By the early 1920s, China was in political turmoil. There were two governments: one in Beijing, known as the Beiyang government, and an alternative 'provisional government' in Guangzhou in the south. The control exerted by both of these was tenuous at best, as regional strongmen and their heavily armed forces regularly rebelled against any authority attempting to control them. Dr Sun Yatsen, the first provisional president of the republic and later the Grand Marshal of the republic, sought help from the West, but his pleas were ignored; the only help came from the recently established Soviet Union. The Soviet representative, Mikhail Borodin, decided to support Sun's KMT on the condition that Sun form an alliance with the CCP. With promises of financial and military aid, Sun Yatsen had little choice but to welcome the CCP into an alliance the KMT, creating what was known as the First United Front in 1923 in an effort to end warlordism in China. Together the KMT and CCP would form the National Revolutionary Army (NRA). However, this 'shotgun wedding' was not to last.

In 1925, Sun Yatsen died, and his military protégé Chiang Kaishek took over the leadership of the KMT. Chiang quickly launched the long-delayed

Northern Expedition between July 1926 and December 1928 to suppress the regional warlords and to unite the nation. Trained by Soviet military advisors, his 'new model army' was immensely successful. Within nine months, half of China had been conquered. But despite the early success – and partly because the KMT itself was equally divided between left-wing and right-wing factions – there were now three centres of power, each proclaiming their city as the nation's capital. The internationally recognized capital of the ROC was in Beijing, while the CCP and left-wing members of the KMT chose the city of Wuhan (located in central China at the Han River's confluence with the Yangtze) as their capital. The right-wing elements in the KMT had their stronghold at Nanjing, and due to Chiang's success in managing the intra-party struggle, this city would eventually become the nation's capital for the following two decades.

The gap between the left-wing members within the KMT was also widening. Chiang decided to solidify his power by purging left-wing members from the KMT, as well as banishing all Soviet military advisors from China. Chiang staged a coup within the KMT party, and in a manner similar to the November 1923 Munich Putsch in Germany, he ordered the execution of many CCP members within the KMT. Many met their end with a knock on the door in the middle of the night, before being shot in the street without trial or investigation.

Mao at this point decided enough was enough, and that henceforth armed revolution would be the only way forward. For many of the surviving CCP members, their initial thinking was to copy the Soviet revolutionary model by fomenting armed insurrections in urban areas; but none were successful. The expected rising tide of urban insurrection did not materialize. Mao tried a different approach, and chanced his arm in rural areas by instigating a peasant farmer-led insurrection (known as the Autumn Harvest Uprising)

A modern depiction of Mao addressing the Gutian Conference (30 October–2 November 1929) in Gutian, Fujian Province. It was here that Mao managed to have a critical concept adopted that still prevails today: 'Military power is subservient to political power' – in this case, the latter being the CCP. Today, the Chinese People's Liberation Army remains under the command of the CCP, and not the state. (Photo12/UIG via Getty Images)

Ruijin, the capital of the Central (or Hunan–Jiangxi) Soviet, which was also known as the Chinese Soviet Republic. Established by Mao in 1930, the Hunan–Jiangxi Soviet provided the Communists with a stronghold where the Red Army could be reinforced and strengthened. The Soviet also offered Mao a social and economic testing ground for peasant-based socialism. It was during his time in Ruijin that Mao Zedong came to the fore as a CCP leader. It also provides an insight into his military tactics and political ideology. (Author's collection)

on 7 September 1927 in his native Hunan Province. It too failed, and he was forced to lick his wounds in the mountains, establishing a key rebel haven in the Jinggang Mountains in Jiangxi Province. Other rebels, such as later Marshal of the People's Liberation Army (PLA – the armed forces of the CCP after 1945) Zhu De, and later Premier of China Zhou Enlai, joined Mao. The stronghold in the Jinggang Mountains (known as the Hunan–Jiangxi Soviet) was not the only rebel-controlled are in China: other similar 'liberated zones' or Soviets could be found in the south-east, centre and south-west of the republic. The common factor was that these areas were highly inaccessible and desperately poor. Mao proved to be a natural leader, and many of these Soviets expanded in size. Moreover, by the early 1930s, the Red Army had expanded its strength to 140,000. While it possessed inferior, and fewer, weapons, the Red Army was often better organized and more motivated than most of the National Army (NA – the military arm of the KMT) at the time.

Naturally, Chiang Kaishek felt threatened by these Soviets and led a series of encirclement campaigns to destroy the Communists. To fund these, Chiang allied himself with gansters and warlords, using the profits earned from opium licences and smuggling. Despite this rich source of funds, Chiang's First, Second and Third encirclement campaigns were all defeated by Mao. However, in the third campaign, a group of foreign-trained Chinese communists returning from the Soviet Union managed to wrestle command of the Red Army away from Mao, and handed it to a three-man committee with Otto Braun, a Moscow-trained German military advisor, playing a central role. However, as a result of the complete domination of the CCP by these 'young Turks', the Red Army lost nearly half its manpower and most of its equipment during Chiang's Fifth Encirclement Campaign. Unable to sustain the losses, on 10 October 1934, the three-man Communist leadership committee formally ordered a general retreat. On 16 October 1934, the Red Army began what later became known as the Long March, fully abandoning the Hunan–Jiangxi Soviet.

CHRONOLOGY

1911

10 October: The Wuchang Uprising begins; it will eventually lead to the end of the Qing dynasty and the abdication of Emperor Puyi on 12 February 1912.

29 December: Sun Yatsen is elected as the first Provisional President of what will become known as the Republic of China.

1912

10 March: Ex-Qing General Yuan Shikai is sworn in as the second Provisional President after forcing Sun Yatsen to step down. Yuan's government becomes known as the Beiyang government.

1916

6 June: Death of Yuan Shikai, and the beginning of the Warlord Era.

1921

23–31 July: Foundation of the CCP.

1926

11 August: Start of the Northern Expedition. It will last until June 1928.

1927

12 April: The Shanghai Massacre – the violent suppression of CCP members by Chiang Kaishek and conservative factions in the KMT.

1 August: Failed uprising in Nanchang led by Zhou Enlai and Zhu De. They will eventually meet up with Mao.

7 September: The Autumn Harvest Uprising, an insurrection led by Mao Zedong attempting to establish the Hunan Soviet. His efforts are short-lived, and he subsequently flees to the Jinggang Mountains.

1930

November: The First Encirclement Campaign against the Hunan–Jiangxi Soviet is launched by the KMT. It will last until January 1931.

1931

April–June: The Second Encirclement Campaign takes place.

July–September: The Third Encirclement Campaign against the Hunan–Jiangxi Soviet.

1933

January–March: The Fourth Encirclement Campaign.

September: The Fifth Encirclement Campaign begins, lasting until October 1934.

1934

16 October: The Central (First) Red Army sets out on its Long March.

Yuan Shikai (in the centre, holding his hat) was formerly a high-ranking general in the imperial Qing government, and plenipotentiary of Korea. He outmanoeuvred Sun Yatsen to become the second Provisional President of Republican China. This picture shows Yuan just after assuming the post on 10 March 1915, at the presidential inauguration reception held inside the Chinese Ministry of Foreign Affairs. On 6 June 1916, 15 months after assuming the presidency, Yuan died from uremia. (Author's collection)

25 November: The Red Army XXV Corps begins its Long March.

1935

15–17 January: At the Zunyi Conference of the CCP, Bo Gu and Otto Braun are sacked, and Mao is rehabilitated.

5–9 February: At the Zhaxi Conference, Mao is passed over for the position of General Secretary in favour of Zhang Wentian.

28 March–14 April: Crossing of the Jialing River by the Fourth Red Army, which joins the Long March.

29 May: The Battle of Luding Bridge.

12 June: The First and Fourth Red armies meet at Maogong (modern Xiaojin County). Mao Zedong and Zhang Guotao disagree on strategy at the Lianghekou Conference (26 June) and agree to go their own separate ways.

20 August: The Mao'ergai Conference; for the first time, Mao proposes the Red Army continue north towards

Shaanxi and Gansu provinces in north-west China, as its final destination.

12 September: At the Ejie Conference, a resolution is passed to reject Zhang Guotao's proposal to lead the Red Army south-west towards the lower Tibetan Plateau.

16 September: Crossing of the Lazhikou Pass. The Red Army XXV Corps ends its Long March and joins up with Red Army forces in China's north-west.

19 October: The First Red Army ends its Long March. The ensuing conference in Wuqi Town reaffirms the location of the new Soviet.

19 November: The Second Red Army embarks on its Long March.

1936

9 October: The Fourth Red Army ends its Long March.

22 October: The Second Red Army completes its Long March.

A model display at the First Party Congress Museum of the CCP in Shanghai. Mao is seen at the rear (fourth from the right). Of the 13 representatives shown here at the first CCP congress, only two would be present at the proclamation ceremony of the People's Republic of China (PRC) 27 years later: Mao Zedong and Dong Biwu (third to the left of Mao). Others became casualties of war, or of the political infighting in the decades that followed. (Author's collection)

OPPOSING COMMANDERS

NATIONALIST

Chiang Kaishek (1887–1975) was a political and military strongman who served as the leader of the ROC from 1928. A close ally of Sun Yatsen, the founding father of the ROC, Chiang rose to fame during the Northern Expedition, but whereas Sun Yatsen was well liked and respected even by the CCP, Chiang Kaishek was not, causing a major split between the Nationalists and Communists that eventually led to civil war. For this, Chiang was accused by his critics of being more willing to conduct a war against fellow Chinese rather than foreign invaders. In the wake of increasing Japanese interference in China, Chiang was taken hostage by his generals in the Xi'an Incident (12–26 December 1936); he reluctantly agreed to an uneasy truce with the CCP after the incident to counter the Japanese threat. Post 1945, the Chinese Civil War resumed, until the eventual defeat of the KMT and Chiang's escape to Taiwan. Chiang Kaishek was never able to return to mainland China, and he died in Taiwan in 1975.

A youthful Chiang Kaishek, in a picture taken during the anti-Warlord Era in the late 1920s. Although Chiang was famous in his later years for his anti-communist stance, before his break with the CCP he was known in the West as the 'Red General'. In his early years, Chiang was in fact pro-communist – so much so that his portrait was regularly featured in Moscow's May Day Parade, carried alongside pictures of Karl Marx, Vladimir Lenin and Joseph Stalin. (Evergreen Pictures)

Gu Zhutong (1893–1987) was a Nationalist general, who in his later years became the defence minister in Taiwan and secretary of the National Defence Council. He participated in the 1911 Xinhai Revolution, and enrolled in the Wuhan reserve-officer academy. In 1922, he joined the staff of the prestigious Whampoa Military Academy (today known as the Republic of China Military Academy). Gu participated in the anti-communist campaigns, and executed his tasks with vigour. In 1941, it was Gu who broke the Nationalist and Communist truce, destroying much of the New Fourth Army (a guerrilla force loyal to the CCP fighting behind Japanese lines).

Bai Chongxi (1890–1966) was a Guangxi Muslim warlord, who later became the ROC's defence minister betwen 1946 and 1948. He was descended from a Persian merchant called Baiderluden, whose offspring adopted the Chinese surname Bai. His Muslim name was Omar Bai Chongxi. During the Northern Expedition, Bai was the chief of staff in Chiang's NRA, and was credited with numerous victories over the northern warlords, often using speed, manoeuvre and surprise to defeat larger

ABOVE LEFT
Johannes von Seeckt came to Shanghai in May 1933 to oversee economic and military development involving Germany in China. He submitted the *Denkschrift für Marschall Chiang Kaishek* memorandum, outlining his programme of industrializing and militarizing China. In the two short years he was in China, he laid the foundations for Chiang's National Army. Von Seeckt can be said to be not only the architect of the Reichswehr (the force that eventually developed into the Wehrmacht) but also the architect of the Chinese National Army, a force that fought almost continuously non-stop from his departure in 1935 to 1949. (Popperfoto/Getty Images)

enemy forces. As the garrison commander of Shanghai, he also took part in the purge of Communists there. Bai left with Chiang for Taiwan in 1949, and ended his days there.

Johannes ('Hans') Friedrich von Seeckt (1866–1936) was a German military officer who served as chief of staff to August von Mackensen in World War I, and was a central figure in the German victories on the eastern front in that conflict. From 1933 to 1935, he repeatedly visited China as a military consultant to Chiang Kaishek. Von Seeckt saved the German military mission by eradicating racist behaviour amongst some of his colleagues: Chiang was so fed up with the arrogance displayed by some of the Germans that he was on the verge of dismissing all the German advisors and engaging French ones instead. It was Von Seeckt who proposed the use of scorched-earth tactics and forcing the Communists to fight in the open, two factors that led to the defeat of the Chinese Communists in the Fifth Encirclement Campaign.

He Jian (1887–1956) participated in many of the Nationalist encirclement campaigns. However, his chief notoriety stems from the fact that he ordered the decapitation of Zhu De's wife Wu Ruolan in early 1929 following her capture in the Jinggang Mountains, as well as the execution of Mao Zedong's wife Yang Kaihui in 1930 by firing squad. He died in Taiwan.

Zhang Xueliang (1901–2001) is better known by his sobriquet the 'Young Marshal'. He was an instigator of the 1936 Xi'an Incident, in which Chiang was held hostage, and forced to agree to a truce with the insurgent CCP and to the formation of a united front against Japan. Zhang was a reluctant participant in Chiang's anti-communist campaigns.

Zhou Hunyuan (1895–1938) was a native of Jiangxi, who joined the Northern Expedition and participated in many of the anti-communist encirclement campaigns with varying degrees of success. His resolute leadership forced Mao to cross the Chi (or Red) River to avoid capture. Zhou died of a brain haemorrhage in 1938 during his tenure as commander of the Tibet–Xikang (modern Yunnan) military district.

Sun Du (1898–1967) and **Long Yun** (1884–1962), both natives of Yunnan Province in south-west China, were warlords who became reluctant generals in Chiang's pursuit of the Red Army through Yunnan. They put little effort into the pursuit, and instead allowed the Red Army to escape from Yunnan. Other rebellious warlords who paid lip service to fighting the Communists include the following. **Wang Jialie** (1893–1966) was chairman of the Guizhou regional government between 1931 and 1935, who cared more about his fiefdom than fighting the CCP; however, Chiang bribed his lieutenants when the Red Army was crossing Guizhou Province, and succeeded in de-militarizing Wang, turning him into a toothless tiger. **Liu Xiang** (1890–1938) was a warlord from Sichuan Province, and another reluctant combatant. The KMT soldiers under his command suffered from low morale, following the heavy attacks by the Red Army, and displayed poor combat effectiveness. General **Wu Qiwei** (1891–1953) was criticized by Chiang for his ineffective suppression of the Red Army. In 1948, he switched allegiance to the Communists and elected to stay in mainland China after the fall of Chiang. **Hu Zongnan** (1896–1962) was one of Chiang Kaishek's most trusted generals, and was one of the very few who participated in all the campaigns of the Northern Expedition. Having graduated from the Whampoa Military Academy in 1924, he spent the following eight years rising rapidly from 2nd lieutenant to major-general, mostly on account of his loyalty to Chiang as opposed to his military skills.

His performance against the Red Army during the Long March was poor, and his troops were routed time and again by Mao's poorly equipped 'bandits'. After 1949, Hu served as a military strategy advisor to the President of the ROC until his death in 1962.

COMMUNIST

Mao Zedong (1893–1976) was the son of a wealthy farmer, and in his early adult life had worked as a teacher and librarian, before rising to become one of the leading figures of the 20th century. His political theories and military strategies have become the stuff of legend in China. Prior to the Long March, Mao was sidelined by the influx of Moscow-educated communists, such as Bo Gu and Otto Braun. He only regained his standing after the Zunyi Conference in January 1935, and his confirmation as the undisputed leader of the CCP was secured at the end of the Long March. Although his political mistakes in the 1950s and 1960s caused great hardship to China, his leadership and ideas led to the creation of modern China, and he continues to be a revered figure in China today.

Zhou Enlai (1898–1976) was the first premier and foreign minister of modern China. Zhou was one of the few Chinese leaders with direct experience of the West, via his travels in Europe, in which he spent time in France, Germany and Britain; prior to this he had also studied in Japan. On his return to China, Zhou joined the Political Department of the Whampoa Military Academy and participated in the Northern Expedition. Zhou was forced to flee Shanghai after Chiang Kaishek's purge of the Communists, and became an outlaw in the wake of his initiating a failed uprising in Nanchang. He made for the hills and joined up with Mao. Zhou's role in the success of the Long March was critical, as he was placed in charge of organizing and supervising the logistics of the long retreat. Unlike many, Zhou survived the purges during the Cultural Revolution (1966–76), and his easy manner made him highly popular with the Chinese public.

Zhu De (1886–1976) was a founder member of the Red Army, who later became a marshal and head of state. Alongside Mao, Zhu was responsible for the creation of modern China. While Mao was the politician, philosopher and strategist, Zhu offered the practical side to the partnership with his excellent military mind. In July 1935, Zhu De and Liu Bocheng (see below) were with the Fourth Red Army while Mao Zedong and Zhou Enlai were with the Central (First) Red Army. Arriving in Yan'an, Zhu De directed the reconstruction of the Red Army under Mao. Zhu survived the Cultural Revolution unharmed, largely due to enjoying Zhou Enlai's protection. Zhu De served in the Politburo until his death in 1976.

He Long (1896–1969) was originally an officer in the NRA, but he rebelled against the KMT when Chiang Kaishek began violently suppressing the Communists. He planned and led the unsuccessful Nanchang Uprising with Zhu De and Zhou Enlai, and escaped capture by hiding in a Soviet in rural south-west China. He Long was forced to abandon his base in one of the encirclement campaigns and joined the Long March only in 1935. He met up with Zhang Guotao, but fell out with him over the strategy of the Red Army, and led his forces to join and support Mao. After 1949, He Long was made a field marshal, and he served as vice premier. Like many of Mao's

Cantonese warlord Chen Jitang was in command of over 300,000 troops, or 30 per cent of the 1 million total Nationalist troops mobilized against the Communist base in Ruijin. However, in reality Chen only deployed 180,000 troops, and furthermore their deployment was not completed until well after the Chinese Red Army had already passed through Chen's territory. Chen made a secret deal with the Communists to allow the Red Army to pass through his region as rapidly as possible, thus eliminating any need for Chiang Kaishek to send troops into Chen's territory and avoiding a potential takeover. (Evergreen Pictures)

early supporters, He Long suffered in the Cultural Revolution, being placed under indefinite house arrest and denied treatment for his diabetes. He was killed by a glucose injection administered by one of his prison guards.

Peng Dehuai (1898–1974) was a prominent Chinese Communist military leader, and served as China's defence minister from 1954 to 1959. Peng was one of the early supporters of Mao in the Jinggang Mountains, and took a leading role in defeating Chiang's first three encirclement campaigns. Peng broke through Chiang's defences in the Fourth Encirclement Campaign and conquered a large area of western Fujian. Of the 18,000 men under Peng's command when the Long March began, only some 3,000 managed to reach safety in Shaanxi in October 1935. Peng would later command Chinese forces during the Korean War, but he suffered in the Cultural Revolution after falling out with Mao, and died in prison.

Otto Braun (1900–74) was born in Ismaning, Upper Bavaria, Germany. He joined the German communist movement in 1921. He later escaped police capture by moving to the Soviet Union and studied at the Frunze Military Academy. In 1933, Braun arrived in Ruijin, at that time capital of the Chinese Soviet Republic, where he became a military advisor on account of his experience in the

Otto Braun, better known by his Chinese name Li De, was one of the few foreigners who managed to take a leading role in the early years of the CCP. Initially, his credentials as a COMINTERN agent advising the Chinese Communists were highly regarded, but Braun proved to be an armchair general only. Eventually stripped of all power in Zunyi, his fall from grace was more than just personal: it had a profound impact on the relationship between the two communist powers. From that moment, the Chinese Communists became increasingly dismissive of any 'helpful' advice given by the Soviet Union. (Author's collection)

Soviet Union. However, Braun proved to be stronger at military theory than field command, and only succeeded in overseeing a fall in the size of the CCP's forces from 86,000 to around 25,000 within the space of a year. At the Zunyi Conference in 1935, Braun was sacked and sidelined until 1939, when he left China for the Soviet Union. He remained there until the death of Stalin, when he returned to Germany to take up various posts, including acting as secretary of the German Writers' Association and as a freelance expert on China.

Bo Gu (1907–46) was one of the 'young Turks' sent to be trained in Moscow. Together with other Moscow-based Chinese, such as **Wang Ming (1904–74)**, he returned to China with the aim of leading the revolution, replacing local revolutionaries like Mao Zedong. Wang and Bo were strikingly alike in many respects: both were representatives of the privileged strata in China's most modern and most Westernized metropolis, Shanghai; Wang was the son of a rich landowner, and Bo the son of a magistrate. Critically, neither had any first-hand knowledge of the Chinese peasantry, nor any political experience. A year after returning from Moscow, at the tender age of 24, Bo secured his leadership of the CCP. His alliance with Braun in the Fifth Encirclement Campaign led to massive defeats that forced the CCP to embark on its great retreat. Bo avoided being purged, mainly because he was willing to confess to his mistakes. He died in an air crash on his way back from attending a CCP meeting in 1946.

Zhang Guotao (1897–1979) was a founding member of and key leader in the CCP, and a rival to Mao Zedong. Zhang was a colleague of Mao's at the Peking University library. In 1931, after the Communists had been driven from the cities, he established the Central (Hunan–Jiangxi) Soviet. When his armies were driven from the region, he joined the Long March, but lost a contentious struggle for the party leadership to Mao Zedong. Zhang's armies then took a different route to Mao's, and were repeatedly defeated. When his depleted forces finally arrived to join Mao in Yan'an, Zhang and Mao failed to make up their differences. Zhang left the CCP in 1938, and defected to the KMT. However, Zhang was not trusted by the KMT either, and given only menial jobs within the party. After the defeat of Chiang Kaishek in 1949, Zhang went into exile in Hong Kong before emigrating to Canada in 1968. In his old age, he lived off the royalties from his memoirs, and died in a nursing home in Toronto.

Ye Jianying (**1897–1986**) was a native Cantonese, and one of the rebels who took part in the Nanchang Uprising in 1927. He became the chief of staff of Zhang Guotao's Fourth Red Army, but critically sided with Mao, and moved north instead of following Zhang's disastrous southern advance. After 1949, Ye was made a marshal, served as defence minister and eventually rose to the largely ceremonial position of head of state, in which he served from 1978 to 1983.

Liu Bocheng (**1892–1986**) participated in the Nanchang Uprising, and served as the first chief of staff of the newly formed Chinese Red Army. After the initial setbacks, Liu travelled to Moscow, learned Russian and attended the prestigious Frunze Military Academy. During the Long March, Liu was appointed as chief of the general staff of the Red Army and was commander of the Central Column, which contained the majority of the CCP senior leadership, such as Braun, Zhou and Mao. Liu stayed out of politics and spent his life in the military, thus avoiding any purges.

Lin Biao (**1907–71**) was a Marshal of China, who played a pivotal role in the Communist victory in the Chinese Civil War, notably in north-east China and during the bloodless capture of Beijing. During the Nanchang Uprising, Lin served as a company commander and later escaped to join Mao and Zhu. Lin was a supporter of Mao's theory of guerrilla warfare, and was regarded as one of the most successful commanders in the Red Army during the Long March. After 1949, Lin held three key posts – vice premier, vice chairman and minister of defence – and was named as Mao's designated successor. Lin died on 13 September 1971, when the Trident jet he was travelling in crashed in Mongolia. The official explanation was that Lin and his family were attempting to flee the country, following a botched coup against Mao.

There were several other notable participants in the Long March, who at the time held junior positions only. **Chen Geng** (**1903–61**) became the chief military advisor to the Viet Minh in the early 1950s. **Liu Yalou** (**1910–65**) later became the first commander of the Chinese Air Force. **Xu Shiyou** (**1905–85**) commanded Chinese forces in the Sino-Vietnamese war in 1979. **Li Xiannian** (**1909–92**) also took part in the Long March, and later rose to become president of China in the mid-1980s.

Lin Biao is regarded as one of the most successful military commanders of the Red Army. During the Long March, Lin commanded the I Corps, considered to be the elite of the Chinese Red Army, chiefly due to Lin's extraordinary talent as a military tactician. According to Edgar Snow, Lin destroyed, defeated or outmanoeuvred every Nationalist force sent against his, and was never beaten in battle. (KEYSTONE-FRANCE/Gamma-Rapho via Getty Images)

OPPOSING FORCES

PRE-1928

During the Warlord Era (1916–28), there were hundreds of militias loyal to whoever paid their wages. Each militia had their own types of weaponry and equipment, and dressed in the manner these warlords saw fit. This was a time of constant change; alliances were formed one day only to be broken the next. This motley collection of armed factions can be classified into the following groups based largely on the area in which they held power:

Major militia groups during the Warlord Era (1916–28)

Anhui Clique	Active 1916–20; controlled northern, eastern and south-eastern China.
Northern (Zhi)	Active 1917–26; controlled Beijing and northern China.
North-East China (Fengtian)	Active 1918–37; led by 'Young Marshal' Zhang Xueliang.
Shanxi Clique	Active in Shanxi Province, north-eastern China from 1911–49.
North-West Army I Corps	Active 1914–30s; originally formed to fight in World War I in Europe.
North-West Army II Corps	Led by Warlord Hu, who changed sides many times, and died in 1925.
North-West Army III Corps	Led by Warlord Sun; like Hu, he kept changing sides, and died in 1928.
Hunan Bandit Army	Formed from Hunan bandits active in southern China; highly unreliable.
Yunnan	Active 1913–27 in southern and south-west China.
Old Guangxi Clique	Active 1911–24 in south-west China.
New Guangxi Clique	Active 1922–53; General Bai Chongxi was a leading member.
Canton Faction	The Cantonese Army in the early 1920s was mostly dominated by Chen Jiongming and later by Chen Jitang, who disposed of Chen Jiongming in a counter-coup. Active 1911–36.
Guizhou Clique	Active 1912–35, with five generations of warlords.
Sichuan Factions	A motley collection of warlords with reputations for poor discipline but fierce fighting ability, despite being badly equipped. Active from the early 1910s to late 1930s.
Zhilu Union Army	A short-lived (1924–28) force featuring exiled 'White' (anti-communist) ex-Imperial Russian Army soldiers fighting as mercenaries.
Five Provinces Union Army	A short-lived (1926–28) force led by General Warlord Sun Chuanfang.
Ma's 'Private' Army	A family-based army with a long history in north-west China, from the mid-19th century to 1949.
Shaanxi Clique	The most famous member was General Yang Hucheng, who was one of the rebels who kidnapped Chiang Kaishek in 1936 in the Xi'an Incident.

Xinjiang Clique	From 1933 to 1944, under the control of General Sheng Shicai, with the sobriquet the 'King of Xinjiang'.
Shandong Clique	General Han defected from the North-West Army and seized power in eastern China.
National Revolutionary Army (NRA)	Chiang Kaishek's new army, trained first by the Soviets then by the Germans. Post-1928 known as the National Army.
Red Army (Soviet zones)	Chinese communists comprising many factions, with Mao Zedong's and Zhang Guotao's being the most prominent.

NATIONALIST

The period leading up to the Long March was a time of change for the Chinese Nationalists. The success of the Northern Expedition had ended the ten-year-long civil war. In theory, China was united, but in a practical sense, the country was still divided into regions where military strongmen ruled supreme. Chiang Kaishek was nominally the head of the country, but his ability to exercise power was limited to the area around the lower reaches of the Yangtze River.

By the conclusion of the Northern Expedition in 1928, Chiang had succeeded in wiping out almost all of the warlords but not the Communists. The Japanese aided this process by dethroning the 'Young Marshal' Zhang Xueliang and his powerful Fengtian Army through annexing the whole of north-eastern China, making it into a Japanese puppet state known as

One of the famous 'turtle-shell' forts built by the Nationalists to create a defensive line that would restrict the movement of Communist forces, and hence access to food and supplies. The success of this line eventually forced the CCP to embark on the Long March. The idea for the forts is commonly attributed to advice given by Johannes von Seeckt, Chiang's military advisor, but some historians, such as Professor Frederic Wakeman, also attribute this to Chiang's reading of Chinese war classics, such as the tactics used by Zeng Guofan in the Taiping Rebellion in 1900. (Evergreen Pictures)

Manchukuo. During this era of consolidation, many of the ex-warlords were absorbed into the NRA, which Chiang renamed as the National Army (NA). New uniforms were issued in 1929, and in 1931 new regulations governing ranks were promulgated with further amendments regarding NCOs, privates, the Navy and Air Force in 1934 and 1935. The 1935 and 1936 regulations were the last to be issued before the outbreak of war with the Japanese in July 1937. The NA in this period was in constant change. The influx of so many different groups from ex-warlord armies brought with it differing customs and loyalties that were not always easy to shake off. Many of the regional troops, especially those from Sichuan in south-west China, were notorious for their opium habits: it was a standing joke that the boys from Sichuan carried two 'rifles' – one for firing bullets, and the other for shooting (i.e. smoking) opium. To create cohesion amongst the NA, Chiang established the Central Officer Training School by reforming the Whampoa Military Academy in Guangzhou and moving it to Nanjing in 1930. At first, it served only to commission 2nd lieutenants, but later, in 1932, a course was added for field officers, which each year saw 500 students graduate. In an army totalling 1 million troops, this was too little to make any significant impact.

Although by early 1930 NA soldiers by and large wore the same uniform, in reality the army was still nothing more than a shotgun wedding of numerous ex-warlord factions, each with differing loyalties, and who only paid lip service to Chiang Kaishek as the supreme leader of China. Rebellion by and disloyalty among regional commanders were common, making Chiang Kaishek highly suspicious and calculating when deploying any troops. The division amongst the many factions within the NA stemmed not only from political divisions but regional differences. China had never been a monolithic society, but instead was a fusion of many nationalities, each with its unique cultures and habits. Furthermore, the fact that many of these ex-warlord soldiers spoke in local dialect meant that a regiment from southern China might not have been able to communicate with a unit from the south-west of the country. On top of the language issue, the newly restructured NA also lacked common standard operating procedures, which made large-scale manoeuvres with other units difficult. Poor inter-unit coordination was a key factor that contributed to the NA's failure in the early anti-communist encirclement campaigns.

According to the 2015 study of the NA by the Chinese academic Zhang Ruide, in 1936 the army comprised, at least on paper, some 177 infantry divisions, 60 independent infantry brigades, 43 independent infantry regiments, nine cavalry divisions, five cavalry brigades and three independent cavalry regiments. In addition, there were four artillery brigades, 18 artillery regiments and 15 more artillery battalions. With regards to support troops, it had two engineer regiments, three transport regiments, two signal regiments and 11 regiments and three independent military police battalions, for a total of 2,029,000 men

This machine gunner, shown firing a Czech-made ZB vz. 26 light machine gun, is from the Nationalist 89th Division and is taking part in an anti-communist encirclement campaign in 1934. Despite being German-trained, the 89th Division was still classified as a second-class unit because it had not completed its transformation to being a fully Germanized division by the outbreak of the Second Sino-Japanese War in 1937. (Evergreen Pictures)

A typical soldier from one of the warlord armies, photographed during the late 1920s. He is seen holding a German MP 18 submachine gun, first introduced into China by the father of the northern warlord Zhang Xueliang, Zhang Zuolin, in the late 1920s. The Qingdao Iron Works was the first Chinese factory to produce the MP 18 locally. (Evergreen Pictures)

(this does not include forces loyal to the Chinese Communists). This echoes a 1937 study of the NA in this period by the American Frederick Field in *Amerasia* (a journal of Far Eastern affairs), which put the NA at 2 million strong, organized into 191 divisions and 56 independent brigades. The NA in the 1930s had a light infantry bias, with hardly any vehicles, guns and least of all armour. In 1935, the best-equipped and most loyal troops, trained by German military advisors, were reported to have had only 457 artillery pieces (excluding mortars – some sources indicate 567 pieces), which equates to only four guns per division. If this represents the best units, the inferior ex-warlord armies would have had virtually no artillery of any kind. The sole exception was the ex-Fengtian forces belonging to Zhang Xueliang, which had some surplus Renault FT-17 tanks, making it one of the first types to be used in China. Other ex-warlord units, such as the North-West Army's I Corps, had several armoured trains. The NA purchased several British Mk VI Carden-Loyd tankettes and later added some 20 Vickers 6-ton tanks. However, none of these tankettes saw action against the Red Army in the Long March, as most of the campaign took place in hilly and mountainous areas.

Within the NA, the best-equipped and most loyal troops comprised some 380,000 first-class soldiers from the I, II, V, VI, XIII, XVI and XXV corps, and the 1st, 4th and 9th divisions, under Chiang Kaishek's direct control. These elite troops were trained by the Germans and armed with the latest German weapons. In addition, there were 550,000 troops classified as second and third class whose reliability was questionable, as many of these were former warlord soldiers forcibly absorbed into the NA.

The reason why the Germans were hired as military advisors grew from a long history of military cooperation between the Prussian and Manchu governments. It is no coincidence that the favourite weaponry of the Chinese came from two major German arms manufacturers, Mauser and Krupp. In the post-World War I period, the military cooperation between Germany

Many of Chiang's NAs soldiers fighting in the anti-communist encirclement campaigns were 'borrowed' from various warlords. Often, they were undisciplined, poorly equipped and essentially little more than bandits in uniform. As seen here, warlord troops typically did not wear helmets, and took little care of their appearance. Transportation means for most of the NA in this period was mainly by mule or horse; only the German-trained troops were equipped with helmets and had access to motor transport. (Roger-Viollet/Getty Images)

and China grew out of the needs of both sides. Weimar Germany was poor and needed extra income, while China found itself continuously at war and was always in need of weapons. Chiang invited the first wave of German advisors in 1927, and with them came German weaponry through the barter and exchange of agriculture products and minerals (needed by Germany for the armament industry). When Hitler came to power, he expanded Sino-German military cooperation, favouring Chiang's anti-communist stance. With the help of the Germans, Chiang planned to reform and re-equip 60 'Germanized' divisions, but this plan was never seen to fruition due to disruption caused by Japan's invasion of China in 1937.

In the NA, the basic military unit was the corps. However, it should be noted that a Chinese corps contained only *c.* 11,000–15,000 soldiers, and most of these were riflemen, with few support troops. By comparison, the Japanese infantry division in the 1930s typically numbered around 12,000 men in peacetime, expanding to 25,000 during mobilization. Problems of quality compounded the deficiency in numbers. Many Chinese soldiers in this period were illiterate, which affected the development of technical arms such as engineering, signals and artillery – and also explains why the NA was so deficient in supporting arms. The lack of money was also problematic. Technical arms are by definition dependent on machinery, which was expensive to import and difficult to manufacture locally. The NA's officers were from the educated classes, but the quality of military education was poor, and the command system was primitive. Even as late as 1937, there were only 2,000 staff officers within the army of 2 million men. Without staff support, the quality of planning and battle preparation was inevitably poor. Furthermore, becoming an instructor in the military academy was seen as a demotion, meaning that good-quality instructors were rare. Much of the learning was done in the classroom, instead of on field exercise, for fuel and ammunition all cost money: a bullet cost the same as 3.5kg of rice or 35 eggs. Thus, training was restricted to only the most basic of soldiering skills.

COMMUNIST

In contrast with the NA, the Chinese Red Army was formed from groups of insurgent fighters, whose only weapons were hand-me-downs and the odd captured rifle. Loosely organized and widely dispersed around the country, the Red Army had humble beginnings; but in the space of three years, by the end of 1930, it was a formidable force of 100,000 men, with 70,000 in the main force and the rest serving in regional and local forces. The main force, however, was not concentrated in one location, but divided amongst ten 'liberated zones' or Soviets, as they were then known. Its rapid growth in the 1930s was partially aided by the devastating infighting between two factions within the KMT: Chiang's NA, and troops loyal to Feng Yuxiang, the former leader of the North-West Army I Corps, supported by other disenfranchised KMT members. The infighting lasted over six months, diverting attention away from the fight against the Communists.

Weapons were often in short supply among Communist troops, and they often had to improvise. At top is a replica of a homemade gun used by the Red Army, or (more probably) by local insurgents within a Soviet. At bottom is a homemade grenade, with a red star logo, and, on the top, a loophole where a cord (usually made of dried grass) was attached. The cord was about 30cm long and aided with throwing the grenade. (Author's collection)

The Red Army was poorly armed, and lacked any formal uniform beyond a simple red star on their caps. Their weapons included swords, spears and homemade weapons such as grenades and even rudimentary flintlocks or muskets – more appropriate to the 19th century than the early 20th. If he was lucky, a Red Army soldier might own a captured weapon, but this was rare in the early days. However, by 1934, just before the Long March, the Red Army had gained a considerable amount of materiel from its three previous encounters with the NA in the first, second and third encirclement campaigns. In some respects, the Chinese Red Army was far in advance of the National Army, for it had understood the importance of modern communications by telephone, telegraph and radio, equipment which most of the Chinese warlord armies still lacked. By the start of the Long March, the Red Army was already regularly transmitting wireless messages in code, and at the same time was breaking Nationalist radio and telegraphic codes.

However, any deficiencies in materiel were more than compensated for by the Communists' good morale and discipline – in contrast to Chiang's NA, many of whom were little more than bandits in uniform. It was in the Jinggang Mountains that Mao first developed much of his military doctrine, including the Chinese Red

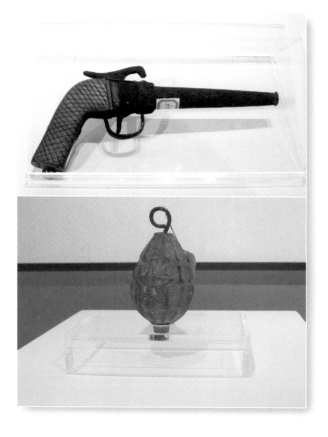

Army's discipline and its respect for civilians. In order to drill this ethos into army, Mao developed the Three Rules of Discipline and Eight Points of Attention – the first military regulations for the Chinese Red Army. The former were:

- Follow and obey orders in all your actions.
- Do not take even a single needle or piece of thread from the people.
- Turn in everything that is captured.

The Eight Points of Attention were as follows:

- Speak politely to all, especially to the people.
- Pay a fair price for what you buy.
- Return everything you borrow.
- Pay for any damage you cause.
- Do not use violence against, or foul language when speaking to, the people.
- Take care not to damage crops and property of the people.
- Do not take liberties with women.
- Do not mistreat any captives.

These rules were made into a song, which all soldiers could sing as they marched, not only to promote esprit de corps but to instil these points into every soldier, even the illiterate. This song has survived into the present PLA; the Viet Cong and the North Vietnamese Army sang a similar (Vietnamese) version. Red Army soldiers would be shot on the spot if they were found looting peasant homes; it was not unknown for a Red Army soldier to leave a coin in the place of a sweet potato he had taken from a farmer's field, as compensation. Such behaviour allowed the Communists to gain the trust of the peasants, who in turn aided the Red Army's war effort by supplying much-needed intelligence, supplies and shelter. Many villagers and their offspring joined the Red Army, providing it with sufficient manpower to fight the KMT, and later the Japanese. In contrast, there were many cases of desertion within the NA, as many soldiers were press-ganged into Chiang's army.

A group of senior officers of the Red Army after their arrival in northern Shaanxi. From right to left: Deng Xiaoping (First Red Army staff), Xu Haidong (Fifteenth Red Army commander), Chen Guang (commander of the 2nd Division, I Corps, First Red Army), Nie Rongzheng, Cheng Zihua (political commissar of the XXV Corps), Yang Shangkun (political commissar of III Corps, First Red Army), Luo Ruiqing (political commissar of I Corps, First Red Army) and Wang Shoudao (secretary of the Politburo, First Red Army). (Evergreen Pictures)

The Chinese Red Army had a unique dual command structure. Every Red Army unit had a political commissar, known as a *zhengwei* (political committee member) at battalion level and above, or a *zhidao yuan* (instructional officer) at the company level. This dual command structure served to ensure the absolute loyalty of the military to its political masters. As Mao once famously said: 'Political power stems from the barrel of the gun.' Many of China's future leaders, such as Zhou Enlai and Deng Xiaoping (1904–97), were once political commissars.

A further unique feature of the Chinese Red Army was that it was a rank-less force. Its soldiers were grouped and addressed by their appointments, for example, 'Regimental Commander Chen' or 'Divisional Political Officer Wang'. Over 80 years later, this tradition persists in the modern Chinese PLA, where it is still common to address the person via his or her job title rather than by rank.

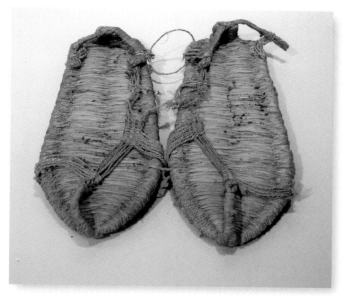

Replica straw sandals of the type typically worn by Red Army soldiers. Many of the regional Nationalist Army soldiers were also still wearing straw sandals even in the late 1930s. (Author's collection)

ORDER OF BATTLE

NATIONALIST

The following ORBAT is for the Chinese Nationalist forces during the Fifth Encirclement Campaign, which was primarily directed at Mao's Hunan–Jiangxi Soviet, and relates to the military situation in January 1934. As the commander in chief of Nationalist forces, Chiang Kaishek established his forward headquarters in Nanchang. In addition to mobilizing the warlords' troops, Chiang also adopted the strategy given to him by his German military advisors Hans von Seeckt and Alexander von Falkenhausen, which involved the systematic encirclement of the Central (Hunan–Jiangxi) Soviet with fortified blockhouses.

After the failure of the Fourth Encirclement Campaign in the spring of 1933, Chiang Kaishek immediately mobilized troops for the Fifth Campaign. The NA troops eventually totalled more than 1 million, mostly forces under various regional warlords, of which the largest part were men from the Guangdong warlord Chen Jitang's army of 300,000 plus. Chen's troops were deployed to the southern border of the Central (Hunan–Jiangxi) Soviet. However, Chen and other warlords were somewhat lukewarm in their attitude towards the campaign, due both to wanting to preserve their power and having already seen four previous campaigns fail. In the end, the majority of warlord troops only participated as blocking forces, and occupiers of the captured Communist regions. The NA troops under Chiang Kaishek's direct command did most of the fighting.

Most of the historical analysis relating to the anti-communist encirclement campaigns in the early 1930s attributes the success of the Fifth Campaign to the advice given by Hans von Seeckt and his military advisors. However, the plan devised by Von Seeckt has remarkable similarities with strategies adopted by the 19th-century Chinese political leader-cum-military commander Zeng Guofan. According to the late Professor Frederic Wakeman Jr. (in his 1975 work *The Fall of Imperial China*), the origins of the successful anti-communist campaigns conducted by Chiang bear the hallmarks of Zeng, who played a key role in suppressing the 1900 Taiping Rebellion (working closely with Charles George Gordon, known as 'Chinese Gordon'). Zeng's strategy was to isolate the rebels from the peasantry and restrict their movement through roadblocks and regular patrolling. Zeng's military exploits were later made famous by Chai E, a Chinese warlord-cum-amateur military historian. Chiang was known to be a vivid reader of Chinese history and must have known about Chai's book, which caused a sensation when it was published in 1911. Thus, when Von Seeckt proposed his plan to Chiang, the latter was already receptive to the idea.

Overall command of NA: National Government Military Commission
Headquarters: Nanchang
Commission Chairman: Chiang Kaishek

NORTHERN FORCE

Commander: Gu Zhutong
Forward Tactical HQ Commander: Jiang Dingwen (later replaced by Chen Cheng)
I Corps (Commander: Gu Zhutong. Reserve Commander: Liu Xing)
1st Calvary Brigade, 2nd Detachment, Tax police (Salt Gabelle) Regiment
93rd Division
27th Division
92nd Division
46th Division
II Corps (Commander: Jiang Dingwen)
1st Detachment (Commander: Wei Lihuang)
    10th Division
    83rd Division

2nd Detachment (Commander: Wang Jingjiu)
    87th Division
    88th Division
Reserve Force
    4th Division
    89th Division
III Corps (Commander: Chen Cheng)
5th Detachment (Commanders: Chen Cheng/Luo Zhuoying)
7th Detachment (Commander: Xue Yue)
8th Detachment (Commander: Zhou Hunyuan)
Reserve Force (Commander: Mao Bingwen)
Strategic Reserve (Commander: Qian Dajun)
13th Division
36th Division
85th Division
23rd Division
28th Division

EASTERN FORCE[1]

Commander: Jiang Dingwen
II Corps (Commander: Jiang Dingwen)
4th Detachment (Commander: Li Yannian)
V Corps (Commander: Wei Lihuang)
9th Detachment (Commander: Liu Heding)
10th Detachment (Commander: Tang Enbo)
Reserve
2nd Detachment (Commander: Wang Jingjiu)

WESTERN FORCE

Commander: He Jian
1st Detachment (Commander: Liu Jianchu)
XXVIII Corps (?)
2nd Detachment (Commander: Liu Yingu)
XXI Corps

---

1   Created out of forces taken from the Northern Force.

Mao (right) is seen here with Zhang Guotao, in Yan'an in April 1938. Shortly after this picture was taken, Zhang defected to the Nationalists. The CCP sent Zhou Enlai and a security detail to arrest him, and they succeeded in apprehending him at Wuhan train station on 11 April 1938. He was given a choice to return to Yan'an or to join Chiang. He chose the latter, and the CCP expelled him from the party and declared him a persona non grata. (Evergreen Pictures)

XVIII Corps
50th Division
19th Division
3rd Detachment (Commander: Chen Jicheng)
36th Division
50th Division
Three infantry brigades

SOUTHERN FORCE

Commander: Chen Jitang
I Corps (Commander: Yu Hanmou)
1st Division
2nd Division
3rd Division
44th Division
Independent 2nd Brigade
II Corps (Commander: Xiang Hanping)
4th Division
5th Division
Independent 4th Division
Independent 5th Division
III Corps (Commander: Li Yangjing)
7th Division
8th Division
Independent 1st Division

ROC AIR FORCE

1st Bomber Squadron
2nd Bomber Squadron
3rd Bomber and Reconnaissance Squadron
4th Bomber and Reconnaissance Squadron
5th Bomber and Reconnaissance Squadron

COMMUNIST

The divisions of the Chinese Workers' and Peasants' Red Army were named according to historical precedence, and not in chronological order. In the early days, Chinese Communist units were often formed through defection from existing NA forces, and retained their original designations. By the time of the Long March, the various small units had been organized into three main groups: the Central (First) Red Army, the Second Red Army and the Fourth Red Army. The Central (First) Red Army was formed from the First, Third and Fifth armies in southern Jiangxi under the command of Bo Gu and Otto Braun, while several smaller units were merged to form the Fourth Red Army under Zhang Guotao in the Sichuan–Shaanxi border area. It should be noted that during the Chinese Civil War, central control of separate Communist-controlled enclaves within China was limited. After the organization of these first two main forces, a further Red Army was formed under the command of He Long, who established his base area in the Hunan–Hubei border zone. However, the defeat of He's forces in 1932 led to a merger of them in October 1934 with the VI Corps, led by Xiao Ke, to form the Second Red Army. These three Red armies would maintain their historical designations as the First, Second and Fourth Red armies until Communist military forces were nominally integrated into the NA, forming the Eighth Route Army and the New Fourth Army, during the Second Sino-Japanese War (1937–45).

At the outset of the Long March, the Chinese Communists were hiding out in various Soviets in China, with Mao's Soviet in the Jinggang Mountains being one of the largest and better organized. A little-known fact as to why Mao was able to achieve better results than other Communist leaders in their Soviets was that Jiangxi Province contained one of the world's largest tungsten mines. Mao was able to secure a significant revenue by cooperating with the Guangdong warlords to export this vital commodity.

However, in October 1934, as the Red Army set off on its retreat now known as the Long March, Mao was a nobody and held no significant position in the Red Army, having been sidelined by Wang Jiaxiang and his group of foreign-educated communists, the 28 Bolsheviks.

The following is the ORBAT of the Chinese Red Army as at October 1934. It should be noted that in this period, there were no standard formations in the Red Army. The terms 'army', 'corps', 'division' etc. cannot be equated with any modern understanding of the terms: a Red Army 'platoon', for example, could consist of anything between 20 and 100 men.

CENTRAL MILITARY COMMISSION

Chairman: Zhu De
Deputy Chairman: Zhou Enlai
Second Deputy Chairman and Political Officer: Wang Jiaxiang
Central (First) Red Army[2] (Commander: Zhu De; Political Officer: Mao Zedong)
I Corps (Commander: Lin Biao; Political Officer: Nie Rongzheng)
    1st Division
    2nd Division
    15th Division[3]
III Corps (Commander: Peng Dehuai, Political Officer: Yang Shangkun)
    4th Division
    5th Division
    6th Division
V Corps (Commander: Dong Zhentang; Political Officer: Li Zhuoran)
    13th Division
    14th Division
VII Corps (Commander: Xun Zhunzhou; Political Officer: Le Shaohua)
    19th Division
    20th Division
    34th Division
VIII Corps (Commander: Zhou Kun; Political Officer: Huang Su)
    21st Division
    23rd Division
IX Corps (Commander: Luo Binghui; Political Officer: Cai Shufan)
    3rd Division
    22nd Division
Second Red Army[4] (Commander: He Long; Political Officer: Ren Bishi)
II Corps (Commander: He Long; Political Officer: Ren Bishi)
    4th Division
    6th Division
VI Corps (Commander: Xiao Ke; Political Officer: Wang Zhen)
    49th Regiment
    51st Regiment
    53rd Regiment
Fourth Red Army[5] (Commander: Xu Xiangqian, Political Officer: Chen Changho)[6]
IV Corps (Commander: Wang Hongkun; Political Officer: Zhou Chunquan)
    10th Division
    11th Division
    12th Division
IX Corpss (Commander: He Wei; Political Officer: Zhan Caifang)
    25th Division
    27th Division
XXX Corps (Commander: Yu Tianyun; Political Officer: Li Xiannian)
    88th Division

Mao with his third wife He Zizhen in Yan'an, shortly after the end of the Long March. Many of the Red Army soldiers took wives with them on the Long March. He Zizhen marched all the way with Mao from Ruijin to northern Shaanxi Province. Mao met her in 1928 in the Jinggang Mountains, and she was highly regarded as an expert in guerrilla warfare and a capable fighter. He Zizhen was also an excellent shot, who earned the nickname of the 'Two-Gunned Lady General'. (Evergreen Pictures)

    89th Division
    90th Division
XXXI Corps (Commander: Wang Shusheng; Political Officer: Zhang Guangcai)
    91st Division
    92nd Division
    93rd Division
XXXIII Corps (Commander: Wang Weizhou; Political Officer: Yang Keming)
    97th Division
    98th Division
    99th Division
Artillery Regiment
Guards Regiment
Peng Yang Political and Military Officer School
XXV Corps[7] (Commander: Xu Haidong; Political Officer: Wu Huanxian)
74th Division
75th Division
Pistol Regiment
X Corps[8] (Commander and Political Officer: Wang Ruci)
XXVI Corps[9] (Commander and Political Officer: unknown)
42nd Division

---

2   Later renamed the First Red Army. Operated in southern Jiangxi and western Fujian provinces.
3   Each of these divisions had three regiments.
4   Operated in Hunan, Hubei, Sichuan and Guizhou provinces.
5   Operated in Sichuan and Shaanxi.
6   Although Xu Xiangqian was the operational commander of the Fourth Red Army, Zhang Guotao exercised political leadership over it.

7   Operated in Hubei, Henan and Anhui provinces.
8   Operated in Fujian, Zhejiang and Jiangxi provinces.
9   Operated in the border area between Shaanxi and Gansu provinces, in north-west China.

OPPOSING PLANS

NATIONALIST

The first colours of the Red Army. The words to the side read (from top to bottom): 1st Division, I Corps, Farmers' and Workers' Red Army. (API/Gamma-Rapho via Getty Images)

Chiang Kaishek's original plan was to destroy the Chinese Communists through the annihilation of their base areas, one by one. The failures of the four previous encirclement campaigns taught the Nationalists valuable lessons, and for the fifth campaign they were supported by a German military advisory team led by the experienced general Johannes von Seeckt. So trusted was von Seeckt that in early 1934 Chiang not only appointed the German as his chief military advisor, but also as the deputy chairman of the Military Affairs Council. In that capacity, Von Seeckt chaired the twice-weekly meetings at Nanjing between Chiang and his most senior generals. It was Von Seeckt who advised Chiang to improve the leadership and command standards within his officer corps by setting up an ad hoc officer training school at Mount Lu. All officers in the Northern, Eastern and Western forces in the Fifth Encirclement Campaign were required to attend a two-week crash course at this institution. (The Southern Force under Chen Jitang was not included, which may explain why the southern section of the Nationalist cordon was where the Red Army managed to break through.) The course was staffed by American, Italian and German instructors, all World War I veterans, and in total 7,598 students passed through the programme.

Von Seeckt also advised Chiang to change tactics, stating that the only way to defeat the Chinese Communists was to conduct a scorched-earth policy, limiting the movement of the rebels and thus their contact with the peasants. It was via the peasants that the Red Army gained most of its intelligence and logistical support, and they served as the cornerstone of Mao's movement. This strategy would also force the Communist guerrillas to

A commemorative stamp issued in 1991 to honour the 90th anniversary of the birth of Xu Xiangqian. Xu was the military commander of the Fourth Red Army. A supporter of Deng Xiaoping, Xu advocated the transformation of the army from a Maoist organization into a disciplined military force. (Author's collection)

fight in the open, where the superior firepower of the NA would offer Chiang an advantage. Following Von Seeckt's advice, in the spring and summer of 1934 the NA built 3,000 'turtle-shell' forts, surrounding the Communist strongholds. A series of protected roads and barbed-wire obstacles linked these forts, thus denying the Red rebels freedom of movement; at the same time, a scorched-earth policy was executed in the areas around the forts in Jiangxi, seeking to eliminate Mao's hideout in the Central Soviet. Furthermore, the Nationalists – for the first time – put time and effort into a 'hearts and minds' campaign, treating the peasantry with greater fairness; Chiang had understood that the insurgency could not be fully vanquished by military tactics alone. It was this strategy, coupled with the errors made by Bo and Braun at the head of the Red Army, that led to a series of defeats suffered by the Chinese Communists, and resulted in the famous Long March commencing in October 1934.

Chiang's 'turtle-shell' strategy would have been successful, save for the fact that he was betrayed by the former warlord Chen Jitang, who commanded the Southern Force in the Fifth Encirclement Campaign. Chen held back his soldiers from harassing the retreating Red Army, believing Chiang was seeking to weaken Chen's Cantonese Army and thus planning to force him from his power base in Guangdong Province. Such was the inter-regional rivalry between Chiang and his former warlord generals that any trust between them was purely skin deep.

As the Red Army moved westwards, Chiang deployed his forces to block a series of possible escape routes. Often many of the regional forces called upon to prevent the Red Army from escaping came from the poor south-western region of China, where loyalty to the central government was minimal and discipline among the soldiers the worst in the entire NA. Both direct disobedience and lacklustre efforts by these regional troops allowed the Red Army to slip through the net time and time again. General Liu Xiang's behaviour in Sichuan Province and General Wu Qiwei's actions in Guizhou Province were typical examples of this reluctance to act. However, not all the warlord armies were so ineffective. The Ma Family Muslim army, which controlled most of Xinjiang Province in the deserts of north-western China, gave Zhang Guotao's Fourth Red Army a good beating. By mid-1935, the Red Army had largely outmanoeuvred the NA by heading into treacherous terrain, such as snow-covered mountain passes at 4,000m altitude, but this did not mean that the Red Army escaped military action. The Red Army had to do battle with rebels from Kham who were fleeing Tibetan government forces in the wake of the failed 1934 Khamba Rebellion.

COMMUNIST

The decision by the Chinese Communists to embark on the Long March was not a pre-planned, tactical move, but one forced on them by the need to retreat in the face of superior enemy forces: the Communists had been defeated not just once, but in almost every battle they had fought since the end of 1932. It was little more than a complete humiliation, fleeing with their tails between their legs and their heads lowered. At the outset, there was no planned route nor even a destination or general direction at which they should aim – it was very much a giant leap into the unknown. After slipping through Chiang's encirclement, it was obvious to the Communist leaders that Chiang was intent on destroying what remained of the Red Army in Hunan, now that the Soviet in the Jinggang Mountains had been abandoned. The Hunan Soviet was the closest Communist base to the Jinggang Mountains, and it was obvious that Hunan would be next on Chiang's list of targets; for this reason, the initial suggestion by Bo and Braun to rendezvous and merge forces with He Long's forces in Hunan was clearly an extremely risky proposition. Mao suggested to Zhou that the Red Army change direction, towards Guizhou, where Mao expected the enemy defences to be weak, but Bo and Braun bitterly opposed this.

Throughout the Long March, the Communist force would convene a series of meetings to determine the direction of movement. It was strategy on the hoof, one step at a time. The first of these meetings took place on 12 December 1934 at Tongdao, a small township close to the border of Hunan and Guizhou in south-east China. Mao and the disenfranchised 'native communists' were growing increasingly angry with Bo and Braun: it was under their leadership that the Red Army had been forced to abandon its bases and strongholds, and, furthermore, in the ensuing two months it had lost a further 50,000 men, reducing the size of the Red Army from 86,000 to barely 30,000. When the Red Army reached Liping, in the mountains of south-east Guizhou, on 18 December 1934, a further meeting was convened. Luckily for Mao, his political rival Braun had fallen ill with malaria, and for the first time Mao had the opportunity to address the gathering. Bo believed that they should travel to eastern Guizhou, but Mao wanted to go to western Guizhou, where he expected the NA to be weak. Mao also thought it better to establish a base area there, instead of walking into a trap by meeting up with He Long's and Xiao Ke's forces. Outvoted, Bo reluctantly had to submit to the collective decision agreed upon, which was to continue westward aiming for a town called Zunyi in western Guizhou, where the most important meeting during the Long March took place. Despite the resolution, Bo and Braun insisted on leading the Red Army towards Hunan to rendezvous with He Long's forces. On the way to Zunyi, an emergency meeting was held in Houchang, and once again Bo and Braun's plans were voted down. From that point onwards, and with immediate effect, all military plans were to be submitted to the Politburo for approval, a practice that continues today in the modern Chinese PLA. The Red Army was now a divided force.

Having pushed out a weak NA force from Zunyi, a meeting was arranged there to examine the causes of the Communists' repeated defeats. This took place in the dining room of a two-storey building belonging to a former warlord. The meeting was a watershed for the Red Army, and resulted in a reshuffling of the leadership of the CCP. Mao managed to shift the blame for the defeat of the Red Army onto the poor tactics and strategies of Bo and Braun. According to Mao, the Red Army was in no position to fight a traditional pitched battle with the much stronger NA. The only way forward was to conduct hit-and-run guerrilla warfare until such a time as the Red Army could be rebuilt within a safe haven. With Zhou Enlai's backing, Mao managed to win over the delegates at the meeting and his motion was carried by 17 votes to three. Bo, Braun and Wang Ming and his clique of 28 Bolsheviks were removed from senior leadership positions and from any military posts with executive powers over the Red Army. Bo and Braun were both relegated to advisory positions with no actual executive power.

Red Army soldiers (squatting) are being questioned by an NA officer after their capture in one of the numerous anti-communist encirclement campaigns. One of the Communist soldiers is carrying a large umbrella on his back. (Keystone-France\Gamma-Rapho via Getty Images)

Prices Set On Heads Of High Red Leaders

Sums Will Be Paid For Capture Of Rebels Dead Or Alive

YOUNG MARSHAL FLIES TO SIAN

Communists' Hardships In Kokonor Told In Graphic Reports

SIAN, Oct. 20.—(Central).—Rewards for the capture of important red leaders, dead or alive, have been announced by Generalissimo's provisional headquarters here today, as follows:

For the capture of

Mao Tse-tung.	alive:	$100,000
	dead:	80,000
Lin Piao,	alive:	$ 60,000
	dead:	40,000
Peng Teh-hui	alive:	$ 60,000
	dead:	40,000
Chow En-lai	alive:	$ 50,000
	dead:	30,000

A reward of $30,000 for the capture alive and $20,000 for the capture dead of any one of the so-called members of the C.E.C. of the bogus Soviet State or commanders of army corps, regiments and divisions of the "Red Army" is also offered.

Nearly all of the Communist rebels had a bounty on their heads, including Mao Zedong, Lin Biao, Peng Dehuai and Zhou Enlai. (Author's collection)

Despite his 'victory' in Zunyi, Mao's control over the leadership was not yet complete. He was passed over for the position of General Secretary at the Zhaxi Conference on 5–9 February 1935, but gained sufficient influence to be elected as one of the three members of the Military Affairs Commission (although subordinate to Zhou Enlai). As the Red Army moved west, debates arose as to whether the force should continue westwards or turn north. In the ensuing discussions, a split developed between Zhang Guotao at the head of the Fourth Red Army and Mao. In a hotly contested meeting held on 26 June 1935 in Lianghekou, Zhang Guotao decided to lead his men deep into south-west China towards the lower reaches of Tibet, while Mao decided to move north. Zhang's forces ended up being massacred by Chiang's, while Mao's expert manoeuvring (doubling back across the Chi River four times, to avoid any contact with the pursuing NA) saved his much-depleted force. Further meetings in August at Shawo, Mao'ergai and Baxi (all within Tibetan tribal areas) confirmed Mao's decision to move northwards in search of a permanent safe haven for the Red Army to be correct, while the Ejie Conference held on 12 September 1935 criticized Zhang Guotao's decision to lead the Red Army south-west towards the lower Tibetan plateau as a mistake. At the Bangluo Town Conference on 27 September 1935, Mao proposed that the safe zone be in northern Shaanxi Province, in north-west China, and not in the south-west.

While the Red Army's plan for the Long March was very much made up as it went along, the tactical doctrine which guided Mao throughout never did change. Mao's combat ethos was guided principally by his now-famous four-line tactical doctrine conceived of while holed up in his rebel hideout, which can be summarized as follows:

The enemy advances, we retreat;
The enemy encamps, we harass;
The enemy tires, we attack;
The enemy retreats, we pursue.

Mao's style of warfare placed the emphasis on fluidity. To quote his words written after the Long March: 'It is to our advantage to recognize this [fluidity in war] characteristic. We must base our planning on it, and must not have illusions about a war of advances without any retreats, or take alarm at any temporary fluidity of our Soviet territory … The strategy of regular warfare is to deny this fluidity.' These two principles guided Mao throughout his life, from his days as a rebel leader in the Jinggang Mountains to routing Chiang in the Civil War in 1949.

THE CAMPAIGN

FROM ENCIRCLEMENT TO FLIGHT

Chiang Kaishek's series of encirclement campaigns sought to root out the rebels from the Hunan–Jiangxi Soviet, with increasing scale and intensity. The first (November 1930–January 1931, featuring 100,000 troops), second (April–June 1931, with 200,000 soldiers) and third (July–September 1931, with some 300,000 men) campaigns ended in failure for Chiang. The Red Army used classic guerrilla tactics to outwit the NA, and moreover, Mao was able to mobilize the people to support the Red Army through intelligence and logistical support. However, with the return of Soviet-educated communists to China, known such as the 28 Bolsheviks, under the leadership of Wang Ming, Mao was sidelined and a Soviet-style strategy was adopted, namely focussing on the capture and dominance of large urban centres. The Fourth Encirclement Campaign (January–March 1933) achieved some early successes, but Chiang's

The Red Army moving off from the Central Soviet. Note the disorganized nature of the army, the lack of proper military equipment, the straw sandals worn; all of these factors made it easy for Chiang Kaishek to underestimate the military capacity of the Communist army. (Archiv Gerstenberg/ ullstein bild via Getty Images)

armies were badly mauled when they tried to penetrate into the heartlands of Mao's Soviet base. During these campaigns, NA columns struck swiftly into Communist-held areas, but were easily engulfed by the vast countryside and were not able to consolidate their footholds.

However, the event that changed Chiang's fortunes, and triggered the Long March, was the Fifth Encirclement Campaign (beginning September 1933). Chiang mustered some 40,000 troops across 23 battalions (the 35th, 42nd, 84th, 86th and 71st divisions, and one independent brigade) and adopted the recommendations of his German advisor Von Seeckt. Instead of mobile warfare, the Nationalists switched to positional warfare, making it difficult for the Communists to shatter and isolate the NA. First, a cordon was placed around the entire Soviet base through the building of a network of blockhouses each linked with barbed-wire and obstacles. Then, gradually the noose was tightened, starving out the Communists. The situation was so grave that by the summer of 1934, two to three months before the start of the Long March, many of the Communist Soviets were running out of salt, an essential part of the diet, and food prices had risen enormously.

Before the decision was taken to abandon the Soviets, the leadership of the Central Soviet (Mao's base) considered other tactics to relieve the pressure on their home areas. One option was to send a Red Army detachment – the VII Corps, comprising some 6,000 troops organized into three divisions – northwards under the pretext of fighting the Japanese in northern China; this would hopefully lure the Nationalists into giving chase, thus weakening the stranglehold on the Soviets. This force would then establish a new Soviet in a liberated area centred on the city of Shangrao, in the border area between Zhejiang Fujian and Jiangxi provinces – which also happened to be in the backyard of a Nationalist-controlled zone, further drawing Chiang's attention away from the Central Soviet. Of the 6,000 men who set off from Ruijin (capital of the Central Soviet) on 6 July 1934, only 4,000 were trained soldiers; the remaining 2,000 were newly drafted recruits. Furthermore, only 1,200 of these 6,000 troops were armed with rifles, and there was only one light machine gun and six light mortars between them. The rest of the troops carried homemade spears and scimitars. Despite being poorly armed, the Red Army VII Corps troops managed to capture 500 cases of Japanese ammunition and 100 precious rifles, and destroyed two companies of local militia loyal to Chiang's government. There were other minor successes as VII Corps advanced, but the main aim of drawing off Chiang's troops from the Soviet stranglehold was not achieved. The VII Corps force managed to survive through into January 1935, but depleted in resources and harassed by superior Nationalist forces, it was eventually wiped out. In hindsight, it is easy to see that it had been sent on a suicide mission, with little hope of establishing a new rebel base, especially in areas where Chiang's power was strong.

The idea of abandoning the Communist Soviets had been first raised in May 1934, when Otto Braun was asked to write a white paper on the options available to the Red Army. By late July, the decision to abandon the Central Soviet was being considered seriously, and on 1 August that year, Mao issued a warning ordering all Red Army units throughout the country to make ready to leave their respective havens and move northwards. Small groups of Red Army troops began to move, ahead of the main force, as early as August 1934; the 2,987 men of the VI Corps under Xiao Ke left the Jinggang Mountains and successfully met up with He Long's forces in October. One of the most contentious decisions regarded who should go and who should stay behind. At one stage, Mao was not included on the list of those taking part in the Long March by Bo and Braun, and were it not for the intervention of Zhou Enlai to include him, the historical record would have been quite different.

On 13 September 1934, the Central Revolutionary Committee ordered all Red Army units to make ready and improve their transport resources, and reorganized its forces into two elements: those who would depart, and those who would stay behind. Non-essential papers were burnt, and printing presses were broken down into parts ready for mule transport. The date for moving out from the Central Soviet was set for mid-October. In order to more effectively gather together this huge force, some 100,000 men plus their equipment formed an advance party, which assembled on the northern banks of the Yudu River from 10 October. The final units arrived on 16 October, and orders were issued to begin crossing the Yudu on the morning of the 17th, at ten separate crossing points. The Long March was now formally underway.

In order to cover the escape of Mao and the Central (First) Red Army, a stay-behind force consisting of a mixture of Red Army troops and local militia, totalling some 16,000 men under Xiang Ying, was ordered to delay the pressing NA.[10] Most of this force was destroyed, and its remnants scattered to seek shelter in western and southern China. Mao's youngest brother, Mao Zetang, volunteered to stay behind, and would be killed in combat in the forest around Ruijin.

Women played a significant role in the Red Army, and many walked alongside men in the Long March. The Central (First) Red Army had 32 women in the Long March; the Second Red Army had 20; the Fourth Red Army had 2,500; and the XXV Corps had seven. Only 350 eventually reached northern Shaanxi. Shown here (left to right) are Chen Congying, Cai Shun, Xia Ming and Liu Ying. (Evergreen Pictures)

Living off the land

The Red Army was now a force on the run, and it would have to live off the land by either capturing supplies from the KMT, local warlords or rich landowers, or seeking help from sympathetic peasants en route. The Red Army would follow a winding, tortuous route, often crossing large areas of barren land, which meant that resourcefulness would be key. Among the items of food consumed would be:

- highland barley flour – one of its staples. Water was added to the flour, and then boiled until stiff. This was formed into a dry, tasteless hardtack that was difficult to swallow and to digest.
- wild roots, grass and bark. Typically, a Red Army soldier carried at

10 When open warfare erupted between the Chinese and the Japanese in July 1937, a second truce between the KMT and CCP (known as the Second United Front) was declared, and Xiang's guerrillas became the nucleus of a new fighting force: the New Fourth Army. This army operated behind Japanese lines and took orders from both the Communist and the Nationalist leadership.

most enough food for two to three days. This often ran out before they reached the next supply point. When this happened, soldiers were forced to eat wild herbs, tree roots and bark, and wild grass to avoid starvation. Some of these wild plants turned out to be poisonous, causing severe vomiting and diarrhoea, and in some cases even death.

- salt, the most critical mineral for the Red Army during the Long March.
- pack animals. When food ran out, horses, mules and other animals were killed and consumed. There were even instances where leather shoes, belts and saddles were boiled up in desperation.
- for water, the Red Army would rely on streams, rivers and rainfall. However, when fresh water was unavailable, its soldiers were forced to drink their own urine, or that of their animals.

Compounding the shortage of food and water, the Red Army troops had to contend with freezing night-time temperatures, inclement weather and agonizing sores caused by walking through mud. Medical supplies would be few and far between.

CENTRAL (FIRST) RED ARMY'S MARCH

A total of 86,859 soldiers began crossing the Yudu River on 17 October 1934. The troops were divided into two field-force columns: the first codenamed 'Red Star', and the second 'Red Seal'. Major Red Army units were also given codenames; for example, I Corps was 'Nanchang', and Third Army 'Fuzhou'. The Central (First) Red Army (consisting of the I, III, V, VIII and IX corps) and Mao formed part of the second Red Seal column. Accompanying the troops leaving the Central Soviet were 15,000 Communist officials and party workers. The combined civilian–military force began heading slowly south-west.

In order to break through the NA cordon, the Communists exploited a weakness in Chiang's forces by secretly holding talks with the Cantonese warlord Chen Jitang, negotiating a truce that would allow the Central (First) Red Army to escape unimpeded through Chen's lines. Chen's greatest fear was not the Red Army, but his losing control of the rich southern province of Guangdong. If the Central (First) Red Army headed south towards Guangdong, the rest of Chiang Kaishek's army would surely follow, and once in Guangdong, Chiang's forces might never leave. Chen therefore quickly reached an agreement with the Central (First) Red Army, which promised not to set foot in Guangdong Province; for his part, Chen would open the defensive lines to allow the Central (First) Red Army safe passage. Whether it was due to poor communication, or being double-crossed by Chen, the Central (First) Red Army's passage through the lines was not smooth, however, and skirmishes took place that resulted in numerous Central (First) Red Army casualties, including a divisional commander. Chen could now at least claim that his forces had tried to stop the Central (First) Red Army, but they were just too strong to prevent escape. Bai Chongxi, the Muslim warlord from Guangxi, had similar ideas. He too deployed his troops in such a way as to deny the Central (First) Red Army entry into his homeland of Guangxi Province, but leaving an open route westwards to allow the Central (First) Red Army to continue their journey. Through luck and good strategic thinking, the Communists exploited the differences between Chen, Bai and

Central (First) Red Army and VII Corps' march

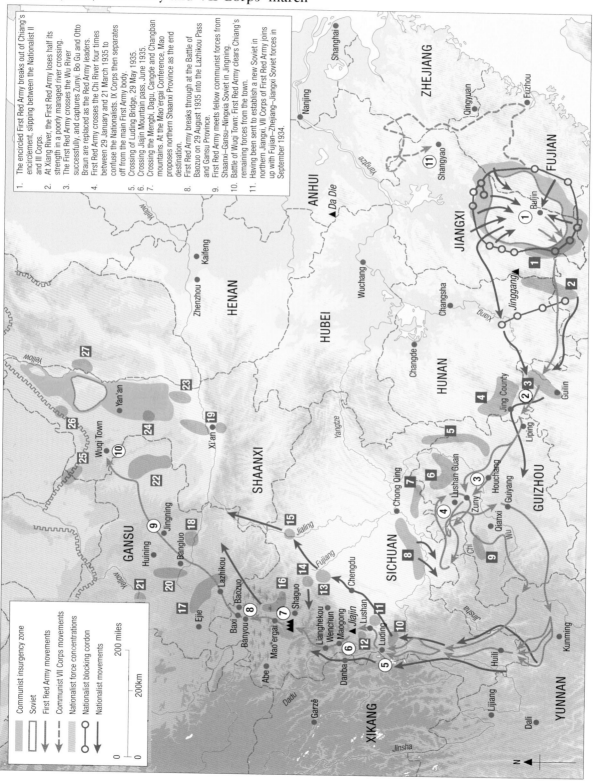

1. The encircled First Red Army breaks out of Chiang's encirclement, slipping between the Nationalist II and III Corps.
2. At Xiang River, the First Red Army loses half its strength in a poorly managed river crossing.
3. The First Red Army crosses the Wu River successfully, and captures Zunyi. Bo Gu and Otto Braun are replaced as the Red Army leaders.
4. First Red Army crosses the Chi River four times between 29 January and 21 March 1935 to confuse the Nationalists. IX Corps then separates off from the main First Army body.
5. Crossing of Luding Bridge, 29 May 1935.
6. Crossing Jiajin Mountain pass, June 1935.
7. Crossing the Mengbi, Dagu, Cangde and Changban mountains. At the Mao'ergai Conference, Mao proposes northern Shaanxi Province as the end destination.
8. First Red Army breaks through at the Battle of Baozuo on 29 August 1935 into the Lazhikou Pass and Gansu Province.
9. First Red Army meets fellow communist forces from Shaanxi–Gansu–Ningxia Soviet in Jingning.
10. Battle of Wuqi Town: First Red Army clears Chiang's remaining forces from the town.
11. Having been sent to establish a new Soviet in northern Jiangxi, VII Corps of First Red Army joins up with Fujian–Zhejiang–Jiangxi Soviet forces in September 1934.

Legend:
- Communist insurgency zone
- Soviet
- First Red Army movements
- Communist VII Corps movements
- Nationalist force concentrations
- Nationalist blocking cordon
- Nationalist movements

0 — 200 miles
0 — 200km

Bo Gu was the nom de guerre of Qin Bangxian, the leader of the 28 Bolsheviks. During the Zunyi Conference, the defection of some critical members of the 28 Bolsheviks (notably Zhang Wentian, Wang Jiaxiang and Yang Shangkun) to Mao's camp led to Bo's downfall. A new military leadership was installed, and Bo Gu lost the post of General Secretary to Zhang Guotao, although he remained a member of the Politburo. (Evergreen Pictures)

Chiang Kaishek, and succeeded in guiding the Central (First) Red Army safely through three defensive lines with only minor losses.

At this stage, the Central (First) Red Army was still under the command of a three-man committee, consisting of Bo Gu, Otto Braun and Zhou Enlai, although the latter had little say in its direction, having been tasked with mundane logistical issues. Bo and Braun's aim was to meet up with He Long's force in the Soviet located where Hunan, Hebei, Sichuan and Guizhou provinces met. However, Chiang had anticipated this; he redeployed his forces to create a series of blocking lines, and ordered his troops to build over 410 'turtle-shell' forts to channel the Central (First) Red Army to a killing zone. Chiang tasked the ardent anti-communist warlord He Jian from Hunan Province with pursuing the Central (First) Red Army.

Although the Central (First) Red Army had avoided any serious clashes with the NA, through bribery and good fortune, by the time it reached the fourth blocking line the Central (First) Red Army baggage-train tail extended back over a distance of 100km. The army could manage only 10–15km a day through the difficult terrain, particularly in hilly and mountainous areas.

Besides being a force of superior quality, the NA had a trump card up its sleeve: air power. Through air reconnaissance, Chiang was able to locate the Central (First) Red Army relatively easily. Knowing that the Central (First) Red Army had no planes of its own, Chiang's pilots began to exhibit unnecessary bravado when strafing the Communists, flying at dangerously low levels. Either through poor piloting skills or lucky shots, the Central (First) Red Army did manage to down a Nationalist plane on 24 November 1934.

On 25 November, the Central (First) Red Army high command finally gave the order to cross the Xiang River in northern Guangxi; if they could cross this before the noose was pulled tight, the Central (First) Red Army could enjoy relative safety, at least for a short while. However, the vanguard only managed to reach the assembly area for the river crossing on the 27th. Knowing that if government forces managed to catch the Reds in the act of crossing the river, it would surely become a massacre, an outer cordon was established to protect the crossing zone. Two regiments from the 5th Division (III Corps) and a troop of mountain guns were tasked with providing the protection. With air support, the NA's 24th Division moved to the attack. Despite the Nationalists almost breaching the line, the Central (First) Red Army defenders held the line in fierce hand-to-hand fighting, but at the cost of some 2,000 men, including almost all their officers. More troops were needed to hold off the NA. The 10th Regiment of the 4th Division (III Corps) lost their commanding officer, and his replacement, all within 24 hours. Despite being supported from the air, the NA did not manage to break through to the river bank, thus allowing the core of the Central (First) Red Army to safely cross the Xiang River. However, the cost to the Central (First) Red Army was 50,000 men, including seven divisional commanders and 16 regimental commanders. Only some 30,000 managed to make it across. Thus ended the Battle of Xiang River.

After the disaster at Xiang River, Bo and Braun increasingly lobbied to join up with the II and VI Corps of the Second Red Army. However, the overwhelming majority of the Communist leadership voted against them.

Mao advocated moving due west into Guizhou Province and allowing the army to recuperate at the town of Liping, where a decision could be taken as to what to do next. A meeting was convened, and the leadership unanimously agreed to move west; a modest reorganization of the Central (First) Red Army was also sanctioned, to compensate for the great losses suffered, amalgamating several units.

In a further meeting at Houchang, Mao advocated a strategy of avoiding combat wherever possible on account of the weakened state of the Central (First) Red Army. However, despite the resolution at Liping not to head towards Hunan to join up with He Long, Bo and Braun ignored this and continued to push to take the Central (First) Red Army there. This would be the final straw for many in the Central (First) Red Army's upper echelons. On 2 January 1935, the Central (First) Red Army set off in a north-westerly direction towards Zunyi, ignoring the directives given by Bo and Braun. The move to Zunyi was relatively uneventful, despite encountering some local militia on the way, which were easily brushed aside. Having overcome the shore defences on the Wu River, the Central (First) Red Army crossed it using

The ROC Air Force provided close air support to the land campaign against the Red Army. Between 1932 and 1936, the Nationalists bought 72 Douglas O-2MC-2 planes (shown here), ten attack bombers and 20 Vought V-92C Corsairs, as well as 24 Heinkel 66 bombers. These airplanes were well suited for counter-insurgency, close air support of the infantry, railway security and punitive raids on undefended villages. Although the Red Army had no air force of its own, it was still able to shoot down a few planes when the pilots flew too low or were careless. (Evergreen Pictures)

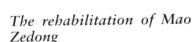

several makeshift bamboo pontoon bridges, a clever manoeuvre that allowed the force to outflank the bulk of the Nationalists. Fear of being surrounded forced many of the Nationalist defenders to abandon their positions and flee to Zunyi. The town was soon captured virtually without loss, thanks to a stratagem straight out of the *Romance of the Three Kingdoms* (a classic of Chinese literature, set in the time of the Han dynasty, AD 169–280), involving the use of captured Nationalist uniforms and banners. At the heart of this deception was the 6th Regiment of the 2nd Division. About ten miles from Zunyi, the regiment captured an entire local warlord battalion and then persuaded their prisoners to act for them (after a few choice words, a few threats and three silver dollars each). After midnight, the Central (First) Red Army arrived at the gates of Zunyi. The Communists and their cooperative captives shouted and chanted, blew their bugles, made a great fuss and proclaimed they were the remnants of a defence battalion being pursued by the Red Army. Within 30 minutes, they were inside the city walls – without a shot being fired. On 9 January 1935, the town of Zunyi fell to the Central (First) Red Army.

The Long March is still very much part of the lexicon of modern China. It is part of the story of the founding fathers of the nation, the story of the nation's heroes, and remains a central element of the education curriculum of every Chinese student. Top left to right: The Glorious Red Armies; The Four Crossings of the Chi River; The Zunyi Conference. Bottom left to right: Setting Off; The Union of the Red Armies; Crossing the Snow-Capped Mountains. (Author's collection)

The rehabilitation of Mao Zedong

In the remote town of Zunyi, in the middle of landlocked Guizhou Province in China's mountainous and ethnically diverse south-west, between 15 and 17 January 1935, a conference took place that would change the course of Chinese history. During this meeting, Mao renegotiated his return to the leadership of the Central (First) Red Army. More importantly, the CCP would abandon the strategy advocated

Liu Shaoqi in his senior years. Liu took part in the Long March, but after the Zunyi Conference he was sent to the so-called 'White Areas' (under the control of the Kuomintang) to organize underground activities. He was based in northern China, around Beijing and Tianjin. Liu later became the Second Chairman (President) of China. (AFP/Getty Images)

by the 28 Bolsheviks, and sanction the sacking of Bo and Braun from all military appointments. The latter were blamed for all the setbacks and suffering endured by the CCP over the previous few years, chiefly the forced evacuation from the Central Soviet and the recent catastrophe at the Xiang River. They were censured for the lack of strategic thinking and direction, poor planning and poor communication with junior commanders, and their dictatorial style of decision-making. On the operational side, the Central (First) Red Army took the opportunity to take stock of its status. To improve rapidity of movement, all the heavy items of equipment (such as the printing machines) were abandoned, and many of the soldiers previously employed as porters were reassigned to bearing arms. The Central (First) Red Army was restructured into 16 regiments, divided into four corps (I, III, V and IX).

News of the Central (First) Red Army's halt at Zunyi soon reached Chiang Kaishek, who immediately ordered more than 150 regiments from all available units to surround the city. But the Communist intelligence network was very effective. There was a brief window when it appeared that the Central (First) Red Army might move northwards to establish a new Central Soviet in northern Guizhou, but with the massing of the Nationalist troops, this had to be abandoned. The only option for the Central (First) Red Army was to move further west into the sparsely populated province of Sichuan. Escape would not be easy, however.

The building in which the Zunyi Conference took place. Zunyi was a turning point for Mao, and a victory for the CCP members whose communist roots lay in China, as opposed to the Moscow-trained CCP members. The Zunyi Conference marked the beginning of the end of the Moscow COMINTERN's influence on CCP affairs. (Evergreen Pictures)

A game of hide and seek

To avoid being trapped in the rapidly closing Nationalist net, the Central (First) Red Army quickly moved out of Zunyi, first heading north and then moving west into Sichuan, crossing the Chi (Red) River. The aim was to seek a crossing point over the mighty Yangtze and re-establish a base somewhere in northern Sichuan. However, Chiang had deployed over 12 brigades of local forces from Sichuan to guard all the possible crossing points, and a search force of three brigades moving south to intercept the Communists. Faced with this situation, the Central (First) Red Army had no choice but to temporarily abandon the crossing of the Yangtze. To avoid being trapped, the Central (First) Red Army turned about and headed back into Guizhou, re-crossing the Chi River, aiming for Zunyi. At the Battle of Zunyi, the Central (First) Red Army gave the four regiments of local militia belonging to Wang Jialie at Lushan Guan (The Gate of Mount Lu) a bloody nose and also destroyed the two weak divisions belonging to Wu Qiwei who had been sent to support Wang Jialie. Five days in the final week of February 1935 witnessed the destruction of two Nationalist divisions as well as a further eight regiments, with 3,000 prisoners being taken. These captives were faced

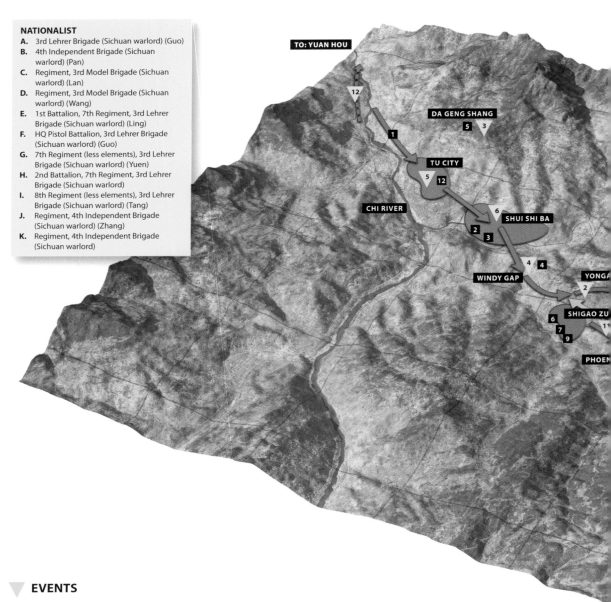

NATIONALIST

A. 3rd Lehrer Brigade (Sichuan warlord) (Guo)
B. 4th Independent Brigade (Sichuan warlord) (Pan)
C. Regiment, 3rd Model Brigade (Sichuan warlord) (Lan)
D. Regiment, 3rd Model Brigade (Sichuan warlord) (Wang)
E. 1st Battalion, 7th Regiment, 3rd Lehrer Brigade (Sichuan warlord) (Ling)
F. HQ Pistol Battalion, 3rd Lehrer Brigade (Sichuan warlord) (Guo)
G. 7th Regiment (less elements), 3rd Lehrer Brigade (Sichuan warlord) (Yuen)
H. 2nd Battalion, 7th Regiment, 3rd Lehrer Brigade (Sichuan warlord)
I. 8th Regiment (less elements), 3rd Lehrer Brigade (Sichuan warlord) (Tang)
J. Regiment, 4th Independent Brigade (Sichuan warlord) (Zhang)
K. Regiment, 4th Independent Brigade (Sichuan warlord)

▼ EVENTS

1. At 0530 hrs on 27 January 1935, the Central Military Commission of the Central (First) Red Army orders the main body of Red Army III Corps (4th and 5th divisions) to occupy Long Xing Chang, with the aim of threatening the concentration of Sichuan warlord armies (3rd Lehrer Brigade under Guo Xunqi and 4th Independent Brigade under Pan Zuo) in Feng Cun Ba (now known as Minhua).

2. Mao sets a trap at Cloud Top by sending a battalion of the Red Army V Corps forward to draw out the Nationalist troops in Feng Cun Ba. At 1400 hrs on the 27th, as the Red Army scouts near the forward positions of the warlord armies, the battalion feigns a retreat, hoping the enemy will give chase. Lying in wait is the Red Army III Corps.

3. Mao sets up his main HQ on the treeless peak at Da Geng Shang.

4. The Tac HQ of the Central Red Army under Liu Bo-cheng is co-located with the HQ of the Red Army V Corps at Windy Gap.

5. The remainder of the Central Red Army Central HQ force is located at Tu City.

6. The V Corps reserve is located at Shui Shi Ba, along with the Central (First) Red Army Officer Cadet Training Regiment under Chen Geng and Song Ren-qiong.

7. The Sichuan warlord army under the overall command of Guo Xunqi pushes forward. He orders the 1st Battalion, 7th Regiment, 3rd Lehrer Brigade (under Ling Jian-xian) to occupy Lion's Peak, which oversees the battle area.

8. The 8th Regiment, 3rd Lehrer Brigade (under Tang Yinghua) clashes with the Red Army V Corps, and, under pressure, is reinforced by 2nd Battalion 7th Regiment.

9. Despite using all of III Corps' artillery and mortar assets to pound the warlord positions, the Red Army is unable to push back Guo's Lehrer Brigade.

10. Around 2000 hrs on 27 January, the warlord army is reinforced by two regiments from the 3rd Model Brigade. The Red Army 4th Division's original plan to attack Feng Cun Ba from the south is scuttled by an unexpected counterattack from a regiment of the 4th Independent Brigade. For the first time since the beginning of the battle, the Red Army is under pressure and on the back foot.

11. Mao intervenes and orders the Officer Cadet Training Regiment, the 2nd Division, V Corps reserves, and elements of the Red Army HQ to counterattack the warlord force, forcing it to retreat. The Red Army sustains some 2,000 casualties; estimated losses for the Sichuan warlord force are similar.

12. Having underestimated the ability of Guo's force, and the number of reinforcements available to it (a luxury the Red Army did not enjoy), on the night of 28 January, the Central Army leadership convenes an emergency meeting, and votes to withdraw from battle and cross the Red River at Yuan Hou.

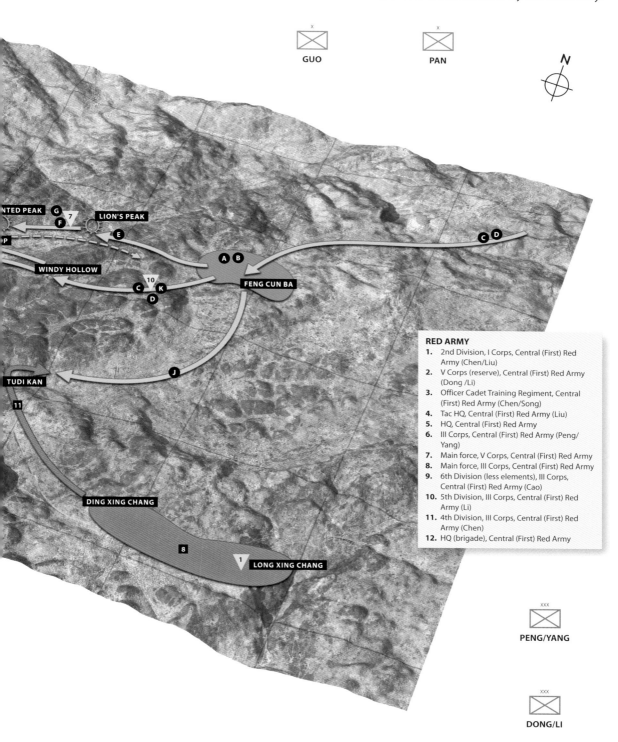

THE BATTLE OF TU CITY, 27–29 JANUARY 1935

The first crossing of the Chi (Red) River by the Red Army.

GUO

PAN

N

PAINTED PEAK · G · 7 · F · LION'S PEAK

P · E

WINDY HOLLOW

C · 10 · K · FENG CUN BA
D

C · D

A · B

J

TUDI KAN

11

DING XING CHANG

8

1 · LONG XING CHANG

RED ARMY

1. 2nd Division, I Corps, Central (First) Red Army (Chen/Liu)
2. V Corps (reserve), Central (First) Red Army (Dong /Li)
3. Officer Cadet Training Regiment, Central (First) Red Army (Chen/Song)
4. Tac HQ, Central (First) Red Army (Liu)
5. HQ, Central (First) Red Army
6. III Corps, Central (First) Red Army (Peng/Yang)
7. Main force, V Corps, Central (First) Red Army
8. Main force, III Corps, Central (First) Red Army
9. 6th Division (less elements), III Corps, Central (First) Red Army (Cao)
10. 5th Division, III Corps, Central (First) Red Army (Li)
11. 4th Division, III Corps, Central (First) Red Army (Chen)
12. HQ (brigade), Central (First) Red Army

PENG/YANG

DONG/LI

During the second crossing of the Chi River, the First Red Army committed the III Corps to capturing the vital Lushan Pass, located just north of Zunyi. (Evergreen Pictures)

with a simple choice: march with us, or die – a method that helped the Central (First) Red Army repopulate its depleted ranks.

In order to lure Nationalist forces to Zunyi, Mao came up with a cunning plan, pretending to stay put in Zunyi while taking the main Communist force westwards to once again cross the Chi River and then head into eastern Sichuan. Chiang believed that the Central (First) Red Army was attempting to cross the Yangtze again, and he ordered his troops to block all the crossing points once more and attempted to ensnare the Central (First) Red Army. Now that the Central (First) Red Army had dispensed with its heavy logistics train, it was able to criss-cross the mountain tracks much more rapidly, and outstrip the Nationalists. The Central (First) Red Army then turned north, and then south-east, re-crossing the Chi River back into Guizhou and returning to Zunyi. This direction of march baffled Chiang Kaishek, and led his forces over south-west China. To further mask its intentions, the Central (First) Red Army then headed south, bypassing Zunyi. The IX Corps then split from the main body and headed back into southern Sichuan. At the same time, Mao ordered a small body of troops to head north-west back towards Hunan, giving the impression that the Central (First) Red Army was attempting to meet up with He Long's troops. Meanwhile, the main body of troops moved south towards the provincial capital Guiyang. Just when Chiang Kaishek thought he had the Central (First) Red Army cornered in Guiyang, the Communists suddenly headed west at a rapid pace, covering more than 60km a day, into Yunnan Province and making directly for the provincial capital Kunming. By now it was clear that the Central (First) Red Army was giving the Nationalists a good runaround.

Despite overwhelming odds against it in terms of troop numbers and equipment, the Central (First) Red Army managed to evade entrapment. In the confused attempts to organize the Nationalist defence of Yunnan, a delivery of maps and other key documents to the newly appointed commander in Yunnan, General Xue Yue, was intercepted by the Central (First) Red Army. With this intelligence coup, Mao immediately gained the upper hand against Chiang, and decided on another unexpected move to outwit the enemy. Just as the Communists appeared to be heading for Kunming, the Reds suddenly turned north and crossed the fast-moving Jinsha River. To secure the crossing points, a small force disguised as Nationalist soldiers tricked the commanders of the local guards in Lugquan, Wuding and Yuanmao into opening their gates, securing a landing point at Longjie without firing a shot. In the meantime, another group marched over 100km to cross the Jinsha River at Jiaoping. Using only seven boats (the smallest of which could carry only 11 passengers) and with the help of local ferrymen, it took the Central (First) Red Army seven days to cross the Jinsha River.

Government troops marching through a town in Hunan during the Fifth Encirclement Campaign. Note the size of a typical Chinese horse, which is generally much smaller than Western or Arabic breeds. (Evergreen Pictures)

The heroes of Luding Bridge

Crossing the Jinsha River was only the beginning: next on the list was the Dadu River, an equally formidable obstacle. Chiang was determined not to let the Central (First) Red Army slip past this time. He ordered the river defences to be doubled, all boats in the area to be confiscated along with food and rations from the riverside communities, and the destruction of

One of the four major crossing points on the Jinsha River, which the First Red Army used. (Evergreen Pictures)

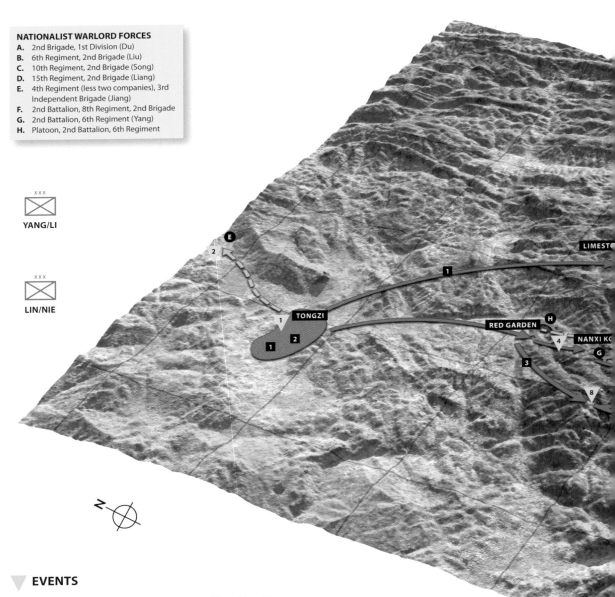

NATIONALIST WARLORD FORCES

A. 2nd Brigade, 1st Division (Du)
B. 6th Regiment, 2nd Brigade (Liu)
C. 10th Regiment, 2nd Brigade (Song)
D. 15th Regiment, 2nd Brigade (Liang)
E. 4th Regiment (less two companies), 3rd
   Independent Brigade (Jiang)
F. 2nd Battalion, 8th Regiment, 2nd Brigade
G. 2nd Battalion, 6th Regiment (Yang)
H. Platoon, 2nd Battalion, 6th Regiment

YANG/LI

LIN/NIE

LIMEST

TONGZI

RED GARDEN

NANXI K

N

▼ EVENTS

1. On the afternoon of 24 February, the leading elements of the Red Army I Corps and III Corps approach Tongzi from the west. The I Corps elements are the first to arrive, and find the town virutally undefended – with only two weak companies of warlord troops guarding it. Without waiting for the main body, the advance elements capture the town.

2. The main body of the Guizhou warlord troops, the 4th Regiment, 3rd Independent Brigade (under Jiang De-ming) have left Tongzi just hours before.

3. The Nationalist 2nd Brigade (under Du Zhao-hua) from the Guizhou warlord army rushes north to defend Tongzi, but by the night of 24 February has only reached the Temple of the Black God.

4. On the morning of the 25th, the Red Army 13th Regiment (under Peng Xue-feng and Li Gan-Hui) from III Corps advances on the west flank towards Red Garden and then to Nanxi Kou. Taking Nanxi Kou is more difficult than expected and fighting continues throughout the night of 25/26 February.

5. Defending the vital Mount Lu Pass is the Guizhou warlord 6th Regiment (under Liu He-ming) with the 2nd Battalion, 8th Regiment as reinforcements.

6. Access to Mount Liu Pass is protected by Nanxi Kou and Mount Dianjin. The Warlord defenders rush additional defenders (10th Regiment, 2nd Brigade under Song Shao-kui) to Mount Dianjin and Limestone Gate. Despite these reinforcements, Mount Dianjin is taken by the 1st and 3rd battalions of the Red Army's 13th Regiment, with support from a platoon of mortars.

7. To prevent reinforcements reaching Mount Liu, the First (Central) Red Army command sends I Corps on an easterly route to occupy Ban Qiao and cut off the Nationalist defenders.

8. With the 13th Regiment held up at Nanxi Kou, the Red Army's 10th Regiment (under Huang Kecheng and Zhang Zong-xun) bypass Mount Liu and head for Little Pointed Hill.

9. Exhausted from its attack on Mount Liu, the 13th Regiment is relieved by the Red Army 12th Regiment (under Zhong Chi-bing and Xie Hao) and conducts mopping-up operations around Mount Liu. Part of the regiment is also directed to capture the Temple of the Black God, thus cutting off any chance of escape by the remaining defenders and ending hope of any reinforcement.

10. The Guizhou warlord 15th Regiment (under Liang Feng-shao) guarding Ban Qiao is ordered north to support the 10th Regiment, but en route meets the panic-stricken defenders from the 10th Regiment on the run. The panic soon spreads across the regiment, and instead of aiding the defence, its troops join the retreat.

11. The Red Army moves rapidly southwards to occupy Zunyi city.

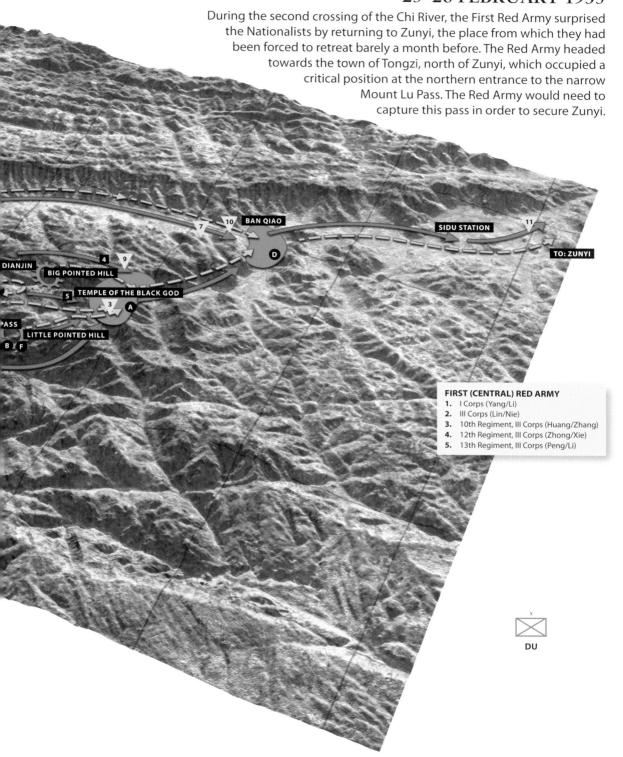

Note that gridlines are shown at intervals of 5km (3.1 miles)

THE BATTLE FOR MOUNT LU PASS, 25–26 FEBRUARY 1935

During the second crossing of the Chi River, the First Red Army surprised the Nationalists by returning to Zunyi, the place from which they had been forced to retreat barely a month before. The Red Army headed towards the town of Tongzi, north of Zunyi, which occupied a critical position at the northern entrance to the narrow Mount Lu Pass. The Red Army would need to capture this pass in order to secure Zunyi.

BAN QIAO

SIDU STATION

TO: ZUNYI

DIANJIN

BIG POINTED HILL

TEMPLE OF THE BLACK GOD

PASS

LITTLE POINTED HILL

FIRST (CENTRAL) RED ARMY
1. I Corps (Yang/Li)
2. III Corps (Lin/Nie)
3. 10th Regiment, III Corps (Huang/Zhang)
4. 12th Regiment, III Corps (Zhong/Xie)
5. 13th Regiment, III Corps (Peng/Li)

DU

47

THE CAPTURE OF LUDING BRIDGE, 24–25 MAY 1935 (PP. 48–49)

In May 1935 the fast-flowing Dadu River (**1**) was swollen by the spring thaw, making the task of crossing it downstream a decidedly risky business. Furthermore, there were only four boats available to the Communists, and Nationalist troops from XX Corps were only five days away and closing fast. This meant that Mao and his force had to cross the Dadu via the only remaining means – the 100m-long Luding Bridge (**2**) – or face annihilation. The bridge, erected in 1706, was built of chains, and it formed a vital link between Beijing and Chengdu, and Chengdu and Lhasa.

At 6.00 am on 24 May, the Red Army coup de main force arrived at the western end of the bridge. After a brief recce by the regimental commander Wang Kaixiang and the political commissar Yang Chengwu, the asault tasks were allocated: the 2nd and 3rd battalions were to provide covering fire, while the 1st Battalion would spearhead the crossing in three waves. The most dangerous task of leading the first wave fell to 22 volunteers from 2nd Company (**3**), with company commander Liao Dazhu leading from the front. The rest of the company formed the second wave,

whose job was to replace the wooden planks on the bridge that had been removed by the defenders (**4**). The 1st Company would form the third wave in the assault.

H-hour was set at 4.00 pm on 24 May. Each of the 22 spearhead volunteers was armed with a submachine gun (**5**), ten grenades and a cavalry sword (**6**) carried on their back. A bugle blast signalled the start of the attack, and they began to edge their way forwards using the 13 chains that formed the skeleton structure of the bridge. To stop the Communists reaching the eastern end of the bridge, some of the wooden boards on the bridge had been left in place by the defenders and were set on fire using paraffin (**7**). The spearhead troops had to make their way through flames, and then began to assault the sandbagged positions guarding the bridge on the opposite bank using grenades. Hand-to-hand fighting ensued with the remaining NA survivors. Just in the nick of time, the Red Army second wave led by Wang Youcai, commander of the 3rd Company, arrived and overwhelmed the remaining Nationalist defenders.

buildings at key defensive points to allow better fields of fire.

Mao came up with a clever plan for the crossing. He decided on a two-pronged attack. The first part involved an eastern column crossing the river by boat. Yang Dezhi, commanding officer of the Red Army's 1st Regiment (1st Division, I Corps), managed to secure the only four boats left afloat within 100km. On 25 May 1935, 17 men, each carrying a submachine gun, a pistol, a scimitar and a few grenades, clambered into these four boats. Supported by gunfire from the southern bank of the river, they stormed the Nationalist positions on the opposite bank without loss, and secured a landing point on the northern bank. However, the journey across the river and back took one hour, and the Central (First) Red Army's chief of staff Liu Bocheng calculated that, at this rate, it would take over a month to ferry the whole Central (First) Red Army across.

This was where the second part of Mao's plan came into play. It involved a coup-de-main force (a western column, consisting mainly of the 4th Regiment, 2nd Division) force-marching

its way to the bridge before storming it. As luck would have it for Mao, on its approach the eastern column defeated all the government troops it encountered on the way to Luding. The NA's brigadier Yuan Guorui fled into the surrounding mountains, and remained there. The lethargic defenders at Luding (comprising the 38th Regiment, 4th Brigade) had spent most of their time sheltering from the bad weather instead of preparing defensive positions to defend the bridge, as they had been ordered to do.

Luding Bridge in the 1970s. Besides the white apartment blocks in the background, little had changed since 1935 when the Red Army crossed this bridge. Note the height of the bridge above the river. (Evergreen Pictures)

The NA's regimental commanding officer, Li Quanshan, had spent more time enriching himself with the profits from selling opium than honing his skills as a soldier. As such, many of 4th Brigade's soldiers were addicts, who needed their daily fix before they could muster enough energy to do anything. Li placed two battalions inside Luding Town, while another battalion was deployed some distance outside in the suburbs. Although on paper the Red Army had numerical superiority, in reality it was an even match as the 4th Regiment had used up its strength during its hurried 24-hour approach march. Approximately two-thirds of the soldiers had fallen behind during the march, and only a battalion-sized force reached the western bank of the Luding Bridge. Knowing the local Nationalist commanders would be found lacking against the Communist forces, Chiang tried to send more capable officers from his officer corps to lead the local troops but this was rejected unanimously by all the Sichuanese warlords. Furthermore, Liu Wenhui, the warlord corps commander at Luding, was open to bribery by the Red Army in return for his non-interference. Besides these political and tactical issues, the weapons of the warlord armies were often inferior to those of the Red Army. Poor

A. Part of the 3rd Battalion, 38th Regiment established a defensive line in the area of Anle Ba to prevent the Red Army from crossing the Dadu River at this point
B. Part of the 3rd Battalion, 38th Regiment established a defensive line at the bottom of Sheep Ring Gully
C. 38th Regiment's main machine-gun and mortar line
D. A company from the 2nd Battalion, 38th Regiment guarded the entrance to the Luding Bridge
E. Main force of 2nd Battalion, 38th Regiment
F. A company of the 2nd Battalion, 38th Regiment

WANG/YANG

MT HAIZI

NANYA KOU

LAMP

SHIANGTIAN BA
ANLE BA

▼ EVENTS

1. Evening of 28 May 1935: the Nationalist Sichuan warlord army's 2nd Battalion, 38th Regiment (4th Brigade, XXIV Corps) is ordered to reinforce Luding.

2. On arrival, the 2nd Battalion, 38th Regiment starts removing planks on the Luding Bridge.

3. The main body of the 38th Regiment (two battalions, with one heavy machine gun and mortar company) arrives at Luding at 0600 hrs on 29 May.

4. 1700 hrs, 29 May: the Nationalist 38th Regiment retreats towards Saddle Mountain.

5. 0600 hrs, 29 May: forward elements of the Red Army's 4th Regiment arrive at the western end of Luding Bridge. The main force (comprising the rest of the 4th Regiment, Officer Cadet Training Regiment and one company of artillery) arrives at noon that day.

6. 0600 hrs, 29 May: part of the forward elements of the Red Army's 4th Regiment moves to capture the high point at Nanya Kou.

7. The Red Army's 4th Regiment's heavy machine gun and machine gun group lays down suppressing fire on the Nationalist troops at Anle Ba.

8. 1600 hrs, 29 May: 22 volunteers of the Red Army start to cross the Luding Bridge. Supported by suppressive fire, these volunteers have managed to cross the Dadu River by 1700 hrs.

9. 1600 hrs, 29 May: the Officer Cadet Training Regiment moves to provide security at Pingshang.

10. A diversionary attack is mounted, feigning to cross the Dadu River by boat.

11. The Red Army's 7th Company crosses the Dadu River by boat.

12. The Red Army's 7th Company races to Luding Town, and attacks the Nationalist defenders at the bridge.

13. By 2100 hrs, 29 May, all of Luding Town has been secured by the First Red Army.

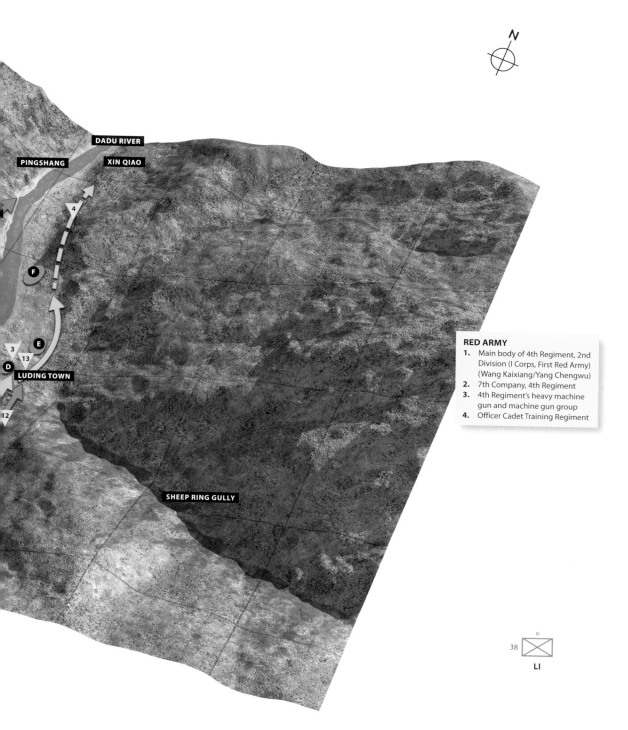

THE CAPTURE OF LUDING, 29–30 MAY 1935

The crossing of the Dadu River played a key role in the Red Army's capture of Luding.

N

DADU RIVER

PINGSHANG

XIN QIAO

LUDING TOWN

SHEEP RING GULLY

RED ARMY
1. Main body of 4th Regiment, 2nd Division (I Corps, First Red Army) (Wang Kaixiang/Yang Chengwu)
2. 7th Company, 4th Regiment
3. 4th Regiment's heavy machine gun and machine gun group
4. Officer Cadet Training Regiment

III
38 ⊠
LI

maintenance was a factor, and lack of training also contributed to a lack of effectiveness. It was said that the warlord's guns were effective at a range of only 100m.

However, the Sichuanese warlord Liu Wenhui was playing a dangerous game, and he needed to be seen doing something: inaction might easily be interpreted by Chiang Kaishek as a sign of collusion with the enemy. So, he ordered many of the planks forming the walkway on the Luding Bridge to be removed, leaving just 13 steel chains spanning the fast-flowing river in the central section.

On 29 May 1935, 22 well-armed volunteers from the Central (First) Red Army's 2nd Company, 4th Regiment (I Corps) crawled across the bare metal chains of the bridge, while under heavy enemy fire. The Nationalist defenders even set fire to the remaining planks as the Communists approached. The 22-strong assault team managed to make it across, driving off the defenders towards Luding town, and secured the vital river crossing point. Chiang's fast-approaching forces failed to reach the bridge in time to take part in the battle. The securing of this escape route for the Central (First) Red Army was critical: without it, Mao's forces would have been wiped out by the rapidly approaching NA reinforcements.

Just prior to the Luding Bridge assault, another coup de main force, comprising 7th Company, 4th Regiment, crossed the Dadu River on rafts some 2km upstream from the bridge. Thanks to a bend in the river, the crossing point was hidden from observation from the bridge, and the Nationalist defenders had placed no sentries at this part of the river bank. The 7th Company troops were thus able to attack Luding town from the rear – and actually fired the first shots in the battle around 2.00 pm. Faced with an attack from both the front and rear, the defenders' morale collapsed, and many fled. Eventually, 60 men from 7th Company succeeded in reaching the eastern end of the bridge, and rendezvoused with the Red Army attackers from 2nd Company. Two hours later, a further bugle call signalled that Luding town and the bridge were in Red Army hands. The Nationalist Army did attempt a counterattack around 10.00 pm, but the attack fizzled out almost before it began as the rest of the eastern column (compring 1st Regiment, I Corps) arrived on the scene.

The casualty count for the battle is unclear; the official account cited only four deaths, while interviews with some of the survivors in the 1990s mentioned 17. One thing is certain: of the 22 spearhead troops who assaulted the Luding Bridge, all made it across safely.

First Red Army's Long March

Start date	10 October 1934
End date	19 October 1935
Distance	c. 12,500km[1]
Manpower at start	86,859 + 15000[2]
Manpower at halfway point	13,800
Manpower at end	7,000[3] + 26,000[4]

Notes:

[1] In a 1936 interview with Edgar Snow, Mao claimed the Long March was 12,500km. This has been called into question by two British researchers, Ed Jocelyn and Andrew McEwen, who in 2003 retraced the route in 384 days (on modern roads) and estimated the distance to be around 6,000km.

[2] Civilians

[3] Those who arrived on 19 October 1935

[4] Stragglers who arrived in October 1936

VII Corps' Long March

Start date	7 July 1934
End date	November 1934
Distance	2,800km
Manpower at start	6,000+
Manpower at end	500+

FOURTH RED ARMY'S MARCH

Around the time when Mao and the Central (First) Red Army were recuperating at Zunyi, the Fourth Red Army under the former Beijing University student Zhang Guotao also began to abandon its Soviet in the mountainous area between northern Sichuan and southern Shaanxi provinces. This Soviet had developed in a similar way to Mao's in the Jinggang Mountains. Founded in November 1933 with some 14,000 troops, despite numerous assaults by Chiang it was able to grow to reach a strength of 80,000, and scored a number of victories against Nationalist warlords, and even downed a Nationalist plane. However, relentless Nationalist attacks between November 1933 and September 1934 meant the troops under Zhang Guotao also suffered significant losses that were hard to make good, while at the same time diverting energy and resources away from farming.

Government forces in pursuit of the Red Army in 1935. Note how little the NA of this period differs from a Napoleonic-era army on the move in the 18th century. (TopFoto.co.uk)

55

Fourth Red Army's Long March

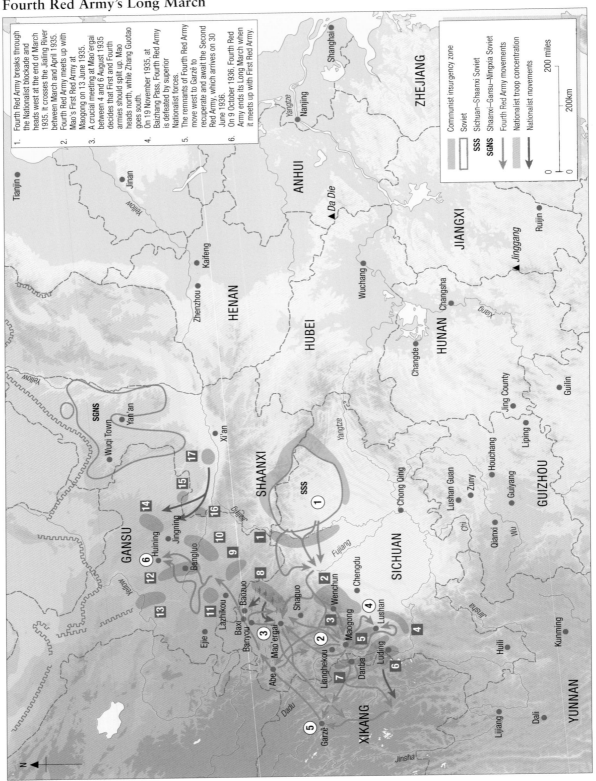

1. Fourth Red Army breaks through the Nationalist blockade and heads west at the end of March 1935. It crosses the Jialing River between March and April 1935. Fourth Red Army meets up with Mao's First Red Army at Maogong on 13 June 1935.
2. A crucial meeting at Mao'ergai between 4 and 6 August 1935 decides that First and Fourth armies should split up. Mao heads north, while Zhang Guotao goes south.
3. On 19 November 1935, at Baizhang Pass, Fourth Red Army is defeated by superior Nationalist forces.
4. The remnants of Fourth Red Army move west to Garzê to recuperate and await the Second Red Army, which arrives on 30 June 1936.
5. On 9 October 1936, Fourth Red Army ends its Long March when it meets up with First Red Army.

Legend:
- Communist insurgency zone
- Soviet
- **SSS** Sichuan–Shaanxi Soviet
- **SGNS** Shaanxi–Gansu–Ningxia Soviet
- Fourth Red Army movements
- Nationalist troop concentration
- Nationalist movements

0   200km
0   200 miles

The lack of food meant the Fourth Red Army was facing starvation, but it also meant that the lack of tax revenue deprived the Soviet's government of much-needed income. The Fourth Red Army was reduced to 60,000 men, and of the original 15 divisions, only 11 now remained.

As Mao's Central (First) Red Army entered Sichuan, a plan was formed to divert attention away from it through a demonstration of force by the Fourth Red Army in northern Sichuan. Xu Xiangqian, the general officer commanding (GOC) of the Fourth Red Army, made probing attacks to the west towards the Jialing River, a fast-flowing tributary of the mighty Yangtze. Despite Chiang's efforts to fortify the key crossing points with two corps (XXVIII and XIX, comprising 53 regiments in total), Xu Xiangqian's army was able to make it to the western side of the river under the cover of darkness. The Fourth Red Army would take a further 24 days to cross the Jialing completely.

Once across, the Fourth Red Army found itself in the resource-rich area on the banks of the Fujiang River, a tributary of the Jialing. The ethnic minorities in the area were receptive to the Communist message, and many decided to join the Red Army there and then. The 28th Regiment (10th Division, IV Corps) was the most successful, gathering over 900 recruits for the Communist colours, swelling the depleted ranks from 800 to 1,700. Soon, Zhang Guotao's army was back to a strength of 80,000 combatants, with a further 20,000 non-combatants (civilian administrators, medical staff, etc.).

Chiang Kaishek correctly anticipated that Zhang Guotao's Fourth Red Army would seek to join up with Mao's First Army in order to establish a new Soviet somewhere in western Sichuan. However, there were no key Nationalist divisions present in the area, and the local forces were wholly ineffective. Furthermore, coordination between the NA and local militias was frought with difficulties. Xu Xiangqian began operations to clear the area in preparation for the meeting of the two Red armies, and, after a series of skirmishes, the illiterate warlord soldiers and their incompetent commanders were soon dislodged by the Red Army.

THE MEETING OF THE FIRST AND FOURTH RED ARMIES

The historic first contact between advance elements of the Central (First) Red Army and the Fourth Red Army took place in Maogong, modern-day Xiaojin County in Sichuan, on 12 June 1935. To reach Maogong, Mao's Central (First) Red Army had to cross the snow-capped Jiajin Mountain (4,930m), and despite being June, the snow was still knee-deep in places. The less physically robust members of Mao's army succumbed to altitude sickness, died of exhaustion or froze to death: few of the troops had adequate winter clothing or footwear. Mao and the Central Red Army's leadership did not reach Maogong until 17 June, and Zhang Guotao only met Mao on the 25th.

To create a degree of uniformity, the Central Red Army was renamed the First Red Army at this point. The combined strength of the two armies now made it a formidable force. More importantly, Mao's army was able to replenish many of the losses incurred over the previous seven months of

THE CROSSING OF JIALING RIVER, 28 MARCH 1935 (PP. 58–59)

As the Mao's Central (First) Red Army entered Sichuan, a plan was formed to divert attention away from it by ordering Zhang Guotao's Fourth Red Army to create unrest in the north of the province. Xu Xiangqian, the operational commander of the Fourth Red Army (under Guotao's political leadership), made probing attacks to the west towards the Jialing River, a fast-flowing tributary of the mighty Yangtze. Despite Chiang Kaishek's efforts to fortify the major crossing points with two NA corps (XXVIII and XIX, comprising 53 regiments in total), Xu's Fourth Red Army troops were able to break through to reach the western banks of the Jialing, tagetting areas where the defences were weakest. Xu organized the first wave in three echelons – left (IX Corps), centre (XXX Corps) and right (XXXI Corps).

In the early hours of 28 March 1935, 50 boats and rafts (1) carrying men from the two battalions from the 263rd Regiment,

88th Division, XXX Corps (2) led the assault against the Nationalist-held positions (3) on the opposite bank of the Jialing River. The noise of the fast-flowing river masked the sounds of the Red Army paddles hitting the water, and the Nationalist soldiers only discovered the Reds when they were right on the shoreline. At a distance of less than 20m, the light machine guns (including Danish-made Madsens, 4) emplaced on the Communists' wooden rafts opened up. The Red Army soldiers (armed with M1888 and Chinese Type 88 rifles, swords, and Mauser C96 pistols, 5) rushed ashore quickly, subduing the stunned Nationalist defenders, many of whom quickly surrendered (6).

The Fourth Red Army would continue crossing the Jialing for a further 24 days, until the whole army had made its way across safely.

hard marching by transferring troops from Zhang Guotao's Fourth Red Army. However, any euphoria was short-lived.

Mao continued to advocate moving northwards to the Shaanxi–Gansu border region, where Gao Gang and Liu Zhidan had established a Soviet, seeking to exploit the anti-Japanese sentiment of the local Chinese which had been growing since the fall of the north-east provinces to the Japanese in 1931. Zhang Guotao considered this to be impractical, and proposed withdrawing to Kham (in western Sichuan) or even into Tibet. Zhang's logic was that, in his view, the south offered a better climate and more plentiful supplies, but Mao's opinion was that in the south the enemy was much stronger, with 130 regiments lying in wait, while to the north lay only wasteland. The terrain might be hard, but at least the Red Army would avoid any serious opposition. More importantly, a march northwards offered a potential location for the CCP to set up a new Soviet. Although both had their reasons, neither was able to convince the other. The seed had been sown that would grow into an eventual splitting of the Reds into two forces.

The Red Army crossing a snowy mountain range. Many of the Red Army soldiers who traversed the high mountains on the Long March lacked adequate cold-weather protection, and succumbed to snow blindness and frostbite as a result. (Universal History Archive/UIG via Getty Images)

Zhang believed that he should be calling the shots: the Fourth Red Army was the larger force of the two, and he led the Fourth Red Army and until recently had also been the chairman of the Sichuan–Shaanxi Soviet – in effect making him the political head of the northern rebel base. Conversely, Mao was still largely an unknown figure, and wielded little real political or military power; he relied on his prestige and his verbal eloquence. Moreover, Zhang had been senior to Mao in the CCP, and joined the party before Mao; now he had no desire to be his subordinate.

In an effort to prevent the impending split, the Central Revolutionary Committee decided to appoint Zhang to the key position of Deputy Chairman of the Central Military Committee. In addition, Zhang was elected as the Chief Political Commissar of the Red Army, in effect handing Zhang control of the First Red Army. On top of this, Zhang was a member of the all-important Politburo and was secretary of the Central Secretariat. However, these olive branches were not enough to placate the increasingly ambitious Zhang. The showdown came at Shaguo in a series of heated debates lasting for two days (4–6 August). Despite some very persuasive arguments, Zhang was unable to convince the attendees to back him.

Maogong, where the First and Fourth Red armies rendezvoused, as seen in the 1940s. Maogong is a Tibetan word meaning 'great accomplishment'. (Evergreen Pictures)

The unified Red Army was now 100,000 strong, and to make this great mass of people more manageable, the commanders agreed to split the force

中國工農紅軍佈告

中國工農紅軍，解放弱小民族；
一切夷漢平民，都是兄弟骨肉，
可恨四川軍閥，壓迫夷人太毒，
紅軍萬里長征，又復妄加殺戮。
苛捐雜稅重重，所有勢如破竹，
今已來到川西，尊重夷人風俗，
軍紀十分嚴明，不動一絲一粟。
糧食公平購買，價錢交付十足。
凡我夷人群眾，切莫懷疑畏縮；
趕快團結起來，共把軍閥驅逐。
誠立夷人政府，夷族管理夷族；
真正平等自由，再不受人欺辱。
布望努力宣傳，將此廣播西蜀。

紅軍總副令朱德

A standing order issued to the First Red Army by Zhu De. Reading from right to left, and top to bottom, the opening lines translate as: 'The Red Army is an army of the farmers and workers; we help the weak to fight the bullies; all races and minorities are our brothers. The detestable Sichuanese warlords are taking advantage of the people, extracting excessive taxes and killing them.' (Evergreen Pictures)

into two: a Right Column under Mao and other 'head north' supporters, and a Left Column under Zhang Guotao's command.

Zhang reluctantly went along with the decision, but from that point onwards the Red Army was in essence a divided force, with Zhang Guotao taking charge of one column and Mao and his supporters the other. Zhang would eventually lead his half of the army where he always wanted to take it, while the Kham rebels and Mao took his force northwards. A mystery remains about the whole affair: why did Zhu De, Mao's trusted military commander, go with Zhang instead of casting in his lot with Mao? The answer can be found in Agnes Smedley's *The Great Road: The Life and Times of Chu Teh* (1956, pp. 120–22), who interviewed Zhu De (or Chu Teh, as she called him) in Yan'an after the Long March. Zhu told Smedley that he was forced to go at gunpoint. Compulsion or pressure there may have been, but it was highly unlikely that this was the whole story. Regional loyalties were a probable factor. After crossing the Jingling River, Zhang's army was replenished by local Sichuanese (which may also explain why Zhang preferred to go south-west instead of north). Zhu De himself was Sichuanese, as was Liu Bocheng: they may have shared Zhang's desire to remain near home territory, where they

held an advantage in language and connections. In any case, there is reason to believe that Zhu was not entirely in agreement with Mao at this point, for he had cooperated with Otto Braun in 1933 and 1934, and pursued a line to which Mao was totally opposed. Mao's choice of a northwards move was eventually proven to be the correct one: Chiang had devised the 'Songpan Battle Plan', which would concentrate 90 regiments to block any Red Army movement eastwards; a further 50 regiments blocking movement southwards; 15 regiments preventing any backtracking towards the Luding Bridge; and 27 regiments blocking movements northwards. General Yu Xuezhong was appointed the overall commander of this 'Anti-Bandit' force.

Zhu De photographed in 1944 in Yan'an, Shaanxi. Zhu was Mao's military mastermind and a loyal supporter during the Long March. Without Zhu's support, Mao may not have been able to regain power within the CCP. Although later in the Long March Zhu was forced to march south with Zhang Guotao's Fourth Red Army (nearly dying in the process), he managed to survive. Recuperating in a Soviet, Zhu oversaw the reconstruction of the Red Army, and it was also under his command that the new Eighth Route Army successfully routed the Japanese in a number of battles, and tied down large numbers of Japanese troops that may have been deployed to other theatres. (From the American Geographical Society Library, University of Wisconsin-Milwaukee Libraries)

Allying with the ethnic minorities in south-west China

As the Red Army moved into south-west China, it began to encounter more and more non-Han Chinese ethnic minorities whose homes lay in the mountains and on the plateaus. Of the 55 recognized non-Han ethnic groups in China, 52 of them can be found in the south-west. Around half of the Long March's route passed through these minority areas. To compound matters, these non-Han minorities were often hostile to the Han Chinese. To guarantee freedom of passage through these areas, the Red Army had to negotiate carefully and sensitively. In Yunnan Province, Liu Bocheng sealed an alliance with the Yi tribe by drinking fresh blood from a recently killed cockerel and swearing allegiance as blood brothers. Donating guns and provisions also helped the Red

Army cause, as did respecting local customs and helping out with farming and other work. This built trust among the ethnic minorities, many of whom ended up joining the Red Army. These minorities also gave vital support to the Red Army, providing intelligence, supplies, helping the sick and injured, and serving as local guides – and sometimes taking part in the fighting, river crossings and bridge building. Without the help of these minorities, the Long March may not have ended in the way it did. However, not all of the encounters with minorities were smooth: the Kham rebels escaping from Tibetan government forces, for example, clashed with both the Sichuan warlord Liu Wenhui and the Red Army during the Long March.

Crossing Songpan

Mao Zedong and his companions in the Right Column still had before them the most harrowing experience of the Long March. In order to bypass the NA, Mao's forces had to attempt to cross what was deemed an impassable, pestilent area of marshy grassland (Songpan) located where Xinjiang and Sichuan provinces converged. Home to swarms of mosquitoes and flies, Songpan lay at 4,000m above sea level; even the local Tibetans considered it impossible to cross. Anyone misplacing their step would become stuck fast, or worse be sucked down into the morass unless fortunate enough to be pulled out by a comrade. Xie Fei, a Long March veteran, recalled in an interview:

> That damned place was very strange – just grass, no trees. It wasn't mountainous, just flat land. It rained every day, and the sun came out every day. The ground was all wet. At first, the vanguard troops sank into the bog. If you tried to pull them out, you would sink too. They couldn't climb out, and they couldn't be rescued either. You could only watch them die. Once we learned this lesson, we let the animals walk first. If the animal sank, then at least the people wouldn't die.

To prepare for the crossing of Songpan, the Red Army ordered everyone to pack 15 days of dried rations, but some could only source two days' worth of food before setting off. A special briefing on how to deal with a Nationalist cavalry attack was delivered to the soldiers, as it was expected that the most likely threat would come from mounted enemy troops.

On 18 August 1935, the Red Army Right Column set off to cross Songpan from Mao'ergai, after a further meeting to confirm the tasks ahead and the general policy of the First Red Army in seeking a haven in the north. Leading the Right Column through the marshland was the 4th Regiment, which had spearheaded the crossing of Luding Bridge. The direction of travel was due north towards the hamlet of Banyou. The Right Column consisted of a mixture of units from the First Red Army (I and III corps) and Fourth Red

Army (IV and XXX corps), and was divided into sections; its vanguard comprised four regiments led by Ye Jianying and Cheng Sicai. On the 21st, the second section comprising the 1st Division (I Corps) under Lin Biao followed. Mao and the senior leadership set off together the next day, along with the remaining troops from the XXX and IV corps. Bringing up the rear was the main body of the I and III corps, together with the staff of the Military Committee. The students and teachers from the Red Army military academy began their crossing on 23 August.

Meanwhile, the Left Column, comprising part of the First Red Army (V and XXXII corps) and part of the Fourth Red Army (IX, XXXI and XXXIII corps) under Zhang Guotao and Zhu De set off from Garzê in a

A Red Army cavalry force in northern Shaanxi. The Red Army did not officially have a cavalry force until it reached northern Shaanxi. Chinese horses generally averaged only 13–14 hands in height. (Evergreen Pictures)

north-easterly direction towards Abe, a Tibetan and Qiang-minority town to the south-west of Songpan. After arriving at Abe, the Left Column moved in a north-easterly direction towards Baxi and Baozuo, at the northern limits of Songpan. To deprive the Reds freedom of movement, Chiang Kaishek had placed guards at these key crossing points, but the greatest concentration of Nationalist forces was in Baozuo. In order to move north, the Red Army would have to take these key crossing points.

On 25 August 1935, the vanguard of the exhausted Red Army completed the crossing of Songpan. No enemy cavalry attack ever materialized, but over 500 of Mao's followers died in the seven days it took to cross the marshland, all of whom succumbed to either sickness or exhaustion. After a brief pause for rest, the First Red Army's vanguard went into action to secure the vital ground of Baozuo.

The Battle of Baozuo, 29–31 August 1935

Baozuo was a nexus of several vital transportation routes. The main and best-constructed buildings in Baozuo comprised two Tibetan temples, defended by 2,700 troops from the 2nd Regiment of Hu Zongnan's Independent Brigade: the Temple of Great Abstinence and its surrounding area was defended by the 3rd Battalion, while 1st and 2nd battalions together with the Regimental HQ was in the smaller Temple of Relief. All the approaches to the small town were defended by pillboxes. As Songpan was considered impassable, Hu placed more of his troops to the south. Hu was shocked to discover that the Red Army achieved the impossible, and on 27 August, rushed the best troops from the 49th Division to the area as reinforcements.

Mao seen here riding a pony in northern Shaanxi. This picture is often dated to the time of the Long March, but Mao has lost his haggard look and has put on weight, indicating that it must have been taken after the Long March when the CCP had established itself in Yan'an in Shaanxi. (Fototeca Gilardi/Getty Images)

Wooden trestle pathways, some only a metre wide, were the only way that generations of Chinese could cross some of the most inhospitable terrain in China. This one is located near Min Mountain in Sichuan. The Red Army marched along this particular pathway in early 1935. (Evergreen Pictures)

Approaching the Nationalists at Baozuo were Fourth Red Army troops under the command of Xu Xiangqian and Li Xiannian. Xu Xiangqian would deploy his force in two halves, one attacking the temples and the other blocking the reinforcements from reaching Baozuo. This would be the final battle that Zhang Guotao's Fourth Red Army would fight in conjunction with Mao's First Red Army, before Zhang's units turned south. Attacking the Temple of Great Abstinence would be the 264th Regiment from the 89th Division (XXX Corps), while two regiments from the 88th Division and two regiments from the 89th Division would form a protective shield on the hills to the north-west of Baozuo to block the approach of Hu's 49th Division. Attacking the more heavily defended Temple of Relief would be the 10th Division (XL Corps). Part of this force would also take control of all the key routes to and from Baozuo, thus isolating the Nationalist defenders. In reserve would be Mao's First Red Army, waiting at Baxi and Banyou.

The battle began at the end of 29 August. The outer pillboxes were easily dealt with, and two companies of Nationalist troops defending the Temple of Great Abstinence were all but wiped out, including the commanding officer. The survivors retreated to the pillboxes on the hill to the rear of the temple and continued to put up a hard fight waiting for reinforcements to rescue them. Anticipating this, Xu Xiangqian decided to lure the Nationalist reinforcements into the hills by not assaulting these pillboxes. On the evening of the 30th, the lead elements of the Nationalist 49th Division, comprising the 291st Regiment, arrived from the south. The Red Army's 264th Regiment (XXX Corps) executed Xu's plan perfectly and feigned a retreat with the aim of luring the attackers deep into the woods northeast of the temple. Lieutenant-General Wu Chengren, the commander of the 49th Division, ordered the 294th Regiment (less the 3rd Battalion) to retake the Temple of Great Abstinence by attacking from the east bank of the Baozuo River, while the 291st Regiment and the 3rd Battalion from the 294th Regiment formed the other arm of the pincer and attacked from the west bank. The 289th Regiment formed the rearguard protecting the 291st Regiment's western flank. The Divisional HQ was in the centre, due south of the temple.

By the afternoon of 30 August, the entire body of the Nationalist reinforcements had been lured into the trap. Around 1500hrs, the Red Army soldiers who had been hiding up in the woods suddenly rushed down from the hills. The Communist 268th Regiment (88th Division) attacked from the western bank and punched a hole through the gap between the Nationalist 291st and 289th regiments, severing contact between the two formations. In less than 30 minutes, the Nationalist forces had been sliced into three parts. First to collapse was the 291st Regiment, and by midnight of the 30th, the entire 49th Division had been routed. Its commander Wu Chengren managed to escape by jumping into the river. Those still hiding in the hills to the rear of the temple saw that all was lost, and surrendered. The Nationalists suffered over 4,000 casualties with a further 800 soldiers taken prisoner. The Red Army captured over 50 machine guns, 5,000 assorted rifles and pistols, and most importantly a vast quantity of food, medical supplies, ammunition and pack animals. On hearing the disastrous news, Chiang Kaishek angrily dismissed Hu Zongnan and Wu Chengren (who managed to make it back alive) as well as General Xue Yue, Hu's superior.

Lazhikou Pass

After breaking through at Baozuo, the I and III corps of the First Red Army were combined into a single force – known as the Shan-Gan Detachment – and continued to proceed northwards. Mao was appointed the formation's commissar and Peng Dehuai its military commander. In total, the detachment had some 7,000 men. But soon their movements were detected by Chiang's air reconnaissance, and he quickly moved reinforcements to the critical Lazhikou Pass, which formed a gateway between north-western Sichuan and southern Gansu.

'Lazhi' is a Tibetan word meaning 'mountain pass', and the pass was located in the Min mountain range inside southern Gansu Province. The pass was flanked by sheer and steep cliff faces on either side towering as high as 500m above the bottom of the ravine, which was filled with a fast-flowing mountain river. The ravine measured a mere 30m at its widest point, and a single narrow wooden bridge spanned the water. Defending Lazhikou were two battalions from the NA's 6th Regiment, 14th Division. Protecting the pass were numerous stone sangars (defensive positions made out of rock) that populated one side of the ravine, allowing the defenders to oversee the critical bridge. These sangars formed strong positions and featured interlocking fields of fire. If the Red Army failed to break through at the Lazhikou Pass, it would mean a massive detour to the west, increasing

An open-topped sangar at Lazhikou Pass. These strong defensive positions provided overlapping and interlocking fields of fire over the vital crossing point, a single wooden bridge that spanned the river at the bottom of the ravine. (Evergreen Pictures)

the ground that they would have to cover as well as the potential for clashing with Chiang's troops. It was a make or break battle, vital to the survival of the Red Army and the CCP.

The critical task of breaking through at Lazhikou was allocated to the 4th Regiment, 2nd Division of the Red Army. This unit first forged its reputation at Luding Bridge. To aid their planning for the attack, the regimental commander Wang Kaixiang and the regimental commissar Yang Cheng-wu conducted a personal reconnaissance of the site, and discovered that not only were many of these sangars devoid of any overhead cover, but the defenders were careless and over-confident and had not deployed sentries guarding their rear. They quickly deduced that if they could get above these sangars and attack them with grenades, they could easily be overcome. The only problem was that the lowest sangar was 80m up, and thus expert climbers would be needed to scale the cliffs without being seen.

One unique feature of the Chinese Red Army was that it was a 'democratic' organization. When battle plans were drawn up, everybody – even a low-ranking private – could contribute and make his point heard. At this critical hour one such private, who was barely 17 years of age, volunteered to climb the sheer rock face with a bag of grenades and to get above the sangars. (History has forgotten his name, and he became known only as 'Yunguichuan', after the three provinces – Yunnan, Guizhou and Sichuan – through which he marched after joining the Red Army.) He was confident that he could lead the way, as he was a good climber, having been raised as a mountain herb gatherer by his father. The coup de main force needed ropes for the climb, but none were available. However, one ingenious soldier suggested tying together their puttees, and quickly a call was made to gather all the puttees from the entire battalion. Soon, two long 'ropes' had been fashioned.

The climb began at dusk, and the men, led by the 17-year-old private Yunguichuan, were armed with extra grenades and a submachine gun each. Yunguichuan was the first to scale the cliff and attached the ropes at

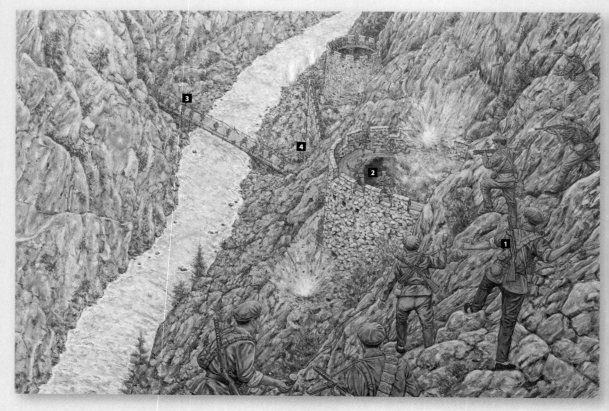

THE CAPTURE OF THE LAZHIKOU PASS, 29–31 AUGUST 1935 (PP. 70–71)

This shows the moment when the Red Army coup de main force (**1**), led by the 17-year-old 'Yunguichuan', attacked the NA defenders in the stone sangars (**2**) from the rear and above, just as dawn was breaking. Grenades have just been thrown down into the sangars, and a few stunned and bloodied NA soldiers are attempting to work out where the surprise attack is coming from.

Meanwhile, down below at the bottom of the ravine, Yang Chengwu's Red Army unit (**3**) is attempting to force its way across the wooden bridge in support of the overhead attack. Yang's men have been pinned down without progress on the bridge for some time. The Red Army troops have now begun a renewed charge, shouting and yelling to gain courage.

Some Red Army troops have already made it across the bridge (**4**), and are about to storm the lower defences. The Nationalist Army troops continue to fire on the Red Army troops coming over the bridge from their sangars.

This is the only bridge that crosses the fast-moving river at the bottom of the Lazhikou Pass. On 16 September 1935, the Red Army crossed from the left to the right and scaled the steep banks to attack the NA sangars located up hillside. A coup de main force scaled the heights behind the sangars, and attacked them from above, throwing grenades down into them. (Evergreen Pictures)

critical points on the cliff face so that the rest of the assault force, including less capable climbers, could scale the sheer cliff. Masked by the darkness and overhanging rock features, they slowly made it to the assembly point above and to the rear of the sangars, ready to launch an attack from this direction. In coordination with Yunguichuan's team, a main Red Army force (comprising 6th Company, 2nd Battalion, 4th Regiment under the command of Yang Chengwu) was waiting at the bottom of the ravine to launch a frontal attack across the single, narrow wooden bridge.

As darkness fell, Yang Chengwu's frontal assault force began its attack by crossing the wooden bridge at the agreed hour, despite not having received the pre-agreed flare signals from Yunguichuan's force. The latter was late getting into its launching off point, as the lead scout had fallen and severely injured himself. Without the surprise rear attack to back it up, the frontal attack ground to a halt.

Just as Yang Chengwu thought that all hope was lost, and as dawn was just about to break, Yunguichuan's assault force finally got into position and fired first a red flare followed by a green one. Better late than never, Yang Chengwu responded with the agreed response of three red flares. With bugles blaring, Yunguichuan's assault troops showered the clifftop positions with grenades and directed their submachine guns into the open-topped sangars. In less than two hours, all the sangars had been destroyed. One of the captured sangars was full of badly needed supplies, to which the Red Army gratefully helped themselves.

ZHANG GUOTAO'S GAMBLE FAILS

Zhang Guotao did not penetrate deep into the marches of Songpan before turning back to Abe, where he held a mass meeting to gain support for his 'southern plan'. This time, Zhang managed to force through a vote denouncing the 'northern plan' as nothing more than a defeatist strategy. On 5 October 1935, in the Tibetan town of Kyom Kyo (modern Jiaomuzu), Zhang convened a closed meeting to formally declare complete separation from Mao's brand of Chinese communism. Stating that he was now the true representative of the Central Committee, and that Mao, Zhou Enlai, Bo Gu and other leaders should be arrested for treachery, Zhang crossed the Rubicon.

Zhang now moved to have Mao and his followers arrested, and if necessary executed, but his plan was foiled by his staff members Ye Jianying and Yang Shangkun, who fled to Mao's headquarters to inform Mao of the plot, taking all of Zhang's codebooks and maps with them. As a result, Mao immediately moved his troops northwards and thus escaped arrest and possible death. With the loss of his codebooks, Zhang now lost contact with the COMINTERN, while Mao was able to establish a link. The COMINTERN gradually began to give greater support to Mao.

On 7 October 1935, Zhang announced his next move, directing his army towards Danba (360km south-west of Maogong), which was captured on 16 October, but at a cost. Maogong fell on the 20th, and Zhang's forces continued towards the south, retracing some of the routes previously used by Mao's First Red Army, albeit in the opposite direction, towards Lushan. The latter fell to Zhang on 12 November.

On 19 November, Zhang came up against a superior Nationalist force at the Battle of Baizhang Pass. The pass was a vital passage towards Chengdu, the capital of Sichuan Province. Chiang gathered a massive force to defend this vital ground, supported by planes and artillery. At the end of seven days' fighting, and despite inflicting over 15,000 casualties on the enemy (for a loss of close to 10,000 men), Zhang's army was forced to withdraw. Adding the casualties sustained over the previous 18 days, Chiang had lost over 40,000 troops, more than half of the Fourth Red Army. While Chiang could rapidly replace men and guns, the Red Army could not.

On 27 January 1936, in a critical meeting at Wayaobao, Zhang finally conceded that his 'southern' strategy should be abandoned. Facing a possible

The Long March remains a popular subject for many artists. This picture entitled 'The Red Army Crossing the Snowy Mountains' is by Ai Zhong Xin, a prominent oil painter, whose work is increasingly collectible. (Photo 12/UIG via Getty Images)

rebellion and with added pressure from Lin Yuying (the CCP's representative to the COMINTERN in Moscow), Zhang reluctantly agreed to turn his army northwards.

Although Zhang's northward route of march did not precisely follow Mao's, the terrain his army had to cross was similar. Zhang had to climb to 3,000m altitude to pass the snow-capped Jiajin Mountain in early March, with the weather still bitterly cold, suffering a number of casualties as a result. In early April 1936, the Fourth Red Army reached Garzê. The army was instructed to recuperate and resupply while waiting for the Second Red Army to arrive (see later). The rendezvous would not occur for two months (30 June 1936), and during this time, Zhang rescinded his claim to absolute power made back on 5 October in Kyom Kyo. The Fourth Red Army would eventually meet with lead elements of the First Red Army on 9 October 1936, officially ending the Long March for Zhang.

Fourth Red Army's Long March

Start date	March 1935
End date	10 October 1935
Distance	c. 5,000km
Manpower at start	80,000
Manpower at halfway point	9,000
Manpower at end	42,764

Liu Chengzhi was one of many self-taught artists who took part in the Long March. This sketch he made after the march for his daughter shows a touching scene he witnessed in Garzê: a Red Army soldier and his wife are bidding farewell to their newborn child. The mother is holding the baby one last time before they separate. (Evergreen Pictures)

THE RED ARMY'S XXV CORPS

The role played by Xu Haidong's and Wu Huanxian's XXV Corps in the Long March also needs mentioning. The XXV began its Long March on 16 November 1934, heading out from the Hubei–Hunan–Anhui Soviet in Anhui Province, central China. Like the First and Fourth Red armies, the XXV Corps was forced from its home territory by a series of massive Nationalist operations, involving over 100,000 troops and similar blocking tactics that gradually starved the Communists out. Prior to the first anti-communist campaigns, the XXV Corps was a force of 12,000 fighters, but the highly effective NA tactics rapidly reduced this down to a mere 3,000 troops. In November 1934, only 2,987 set off from the Soviet. Although nominally a corps, it had only three regiments, the 223rd, 224th and 225th, plus a roughly battalion-sized unit of troops armed only with Mauser C96 semi-automatic pistols, or similar handguns (known collectively as the Pistol Regiment). As happened in other Soviets, a stay-behind force remained to delay any NA pursuit.

The XXV's decision to break out was in part encouraged by Zhou Enlai's letter outlining the decision by the Central Revolutionary Committee to seek

Red Army XXV Corps' Long March

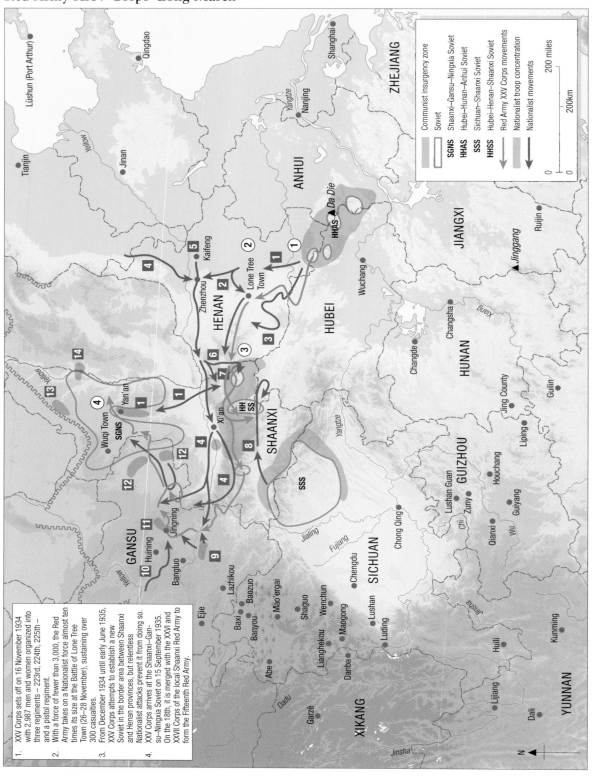

1. XXV Corps sets off on 16 November 1934 with 2,987 men and women organized into three regiments – 223rd, 224th, 225th – and a pistol regiment.
2. With a force of fewer than 3,000, the Red Army takes on a Nationalist force almost ten times its size at the Battle of Lone Tree Town (26–28 November), sustaining over 300 casualties.
3. From December 1934 until early June 1935, XXV Corps attempts to establish a new Soviet in the border area between Shaanxi and Henan provinces, but relentless Nationalist attacks prevent it from doing so.
4. XXV Corps arrives at the Shaanxi-Gan-su–Ningxia Soviet on 15 September 1935. On the 18th, it is merged with the XXVI and XXVII Corps of the local Shaanxi Red Army to form the Fifteenth Red Army.

Two Red Army soldiers in Yan'an shortly after the end of the Long March. This state of dress is typical of a Red Army soldier at the end of the Long March. The uniforms, although made of poor-quality material, at least are now showing a degree of uniformity. Their personal equipment remains unstandardized, and their shoes (for those that had them) were either made of straw or canvas. Both of these soldiers are linesmen. (From the American Geographical Society Library, University of Wisconsin-Milwaukee Libraries)

OPPOSITE
Key to Nationalist units
1. LXVII Corps
2. 95th Division
3. XL Corps
4. LI Corps
5. III Corps
6. 60th Division
7. 95th Division
8. 1st, 2nd, 3rd brigades
9. 12th Division
10. 17th Brigade
11. 11th Brigade
12. 35th Division
13. 86th Division
14. 2nd Brigade (101st Division), 206th Brigade (71st Division), 208th Brigade (72nd Division)

alternative base areas. On 11 November 1934, after an all-night meeting, the decision to abandon the Hubei–Hunan–Anhui Soviet was confirmed, with a direction of travel north-west, where Chiang's forces were weakest. Unlike the First Red Army in its initial phase, the XXV Corps travelled light, with each soldier ordered to carry 'three days' rations and two pairs of straw sandals'. Its first objective was Tongbo Mountain on the border between Hubei and Henan provinces, where the XXV only narrowly escaped extermination thanks to pro-Communist villagers who warned them of NA troops in the villages that lay ahead. Despite its lucky escape, the XXV Corps

Not all the Red Army's soldiers took part in the Long March. Only the fittest and most capable were selected. Furthermore, some were ordered to stay behind in the Soviets to delay the NA; many of these were captured. Seen here is a 'welcome' gathering for a former Red Army soldier who is now swearing allegiance to Chiang Kaishek. (Evergreen Pictures)

was not out of trouble; the Nationalists were still hot on their heels. However, once again the Communists outsmarted the pursuing NA by turning south and feigning an attack on Zaoyang County, giving the impression that the Reds would then attack Wuhan, a key city in Hubei Province in central China. Just before the NA troops arrived, the XXV Corps doubled back on itself and moved north towards Lone Tree Town in Henan Province.

The Battle of Lone Tree Town

If the First Red Army's reputation was sealed by the Battle of Luding Bridge, for the XXV Corps it was the Battle of Lone Tree Town. On 25 November 1934, the pursuing NA was closing fast on the corps. The Nationalists deployed their three cavalry regiments from the 2nd Anti-Bandit Detachment ahead of the main force, and these mounted troops soon clashed with the rear column of the Communist 225th Regiment. Despite sustaining 100 casualties, the Red defensive line held. Relieved by the 223rd Regiment, both the 224th and 225th regiments headed rapidly for the hills, trying to escape encirclement. The poor visibility and snow showers helped conceal the escaping corps. However, this was to become a double-edged sword: while the snow hid the Communists, it also made the Communists less aware of the dangers around them. The advance guard of the 224th Regiment was suddenly hit by a hail of bullets as it approached Lone Tree Town. Three regiments from the NA's 116th Division, as well as its divisional reconnaissance unit and cavalry regiment, were lying in wait. The XXV Corps troops were caught in the open with little cover, and the low temperature froze many of the weapons solid, preventing the men from the 224th Regiment from returning fire. Seeing a golden opportunity, the Nationalist troops charged, trying to outflank the Communists, but the 224th managed to escape encirclement by retreating some 5km into a hamlet whose name has been lost to history. There they managed to recuperate briefly as the unit commanders attempted to find a way out. In the nick of time, the 3rd Battalion from the 225th Regiment came to the rescue and held off the repeated attacks by the NA, while a group of some 60–70 men from the Pistol Regiment attempted to find a way of breaking out. They succeeded in locating a track between the NA lines and escaped under the cover of the falling snow and poor visibility onto the eastern slopes of the densely wooded Funiu Mountain.

Until this point, the XXV Corps had no real idea where it was heading, except knowing that north-west was the preferred direction, as

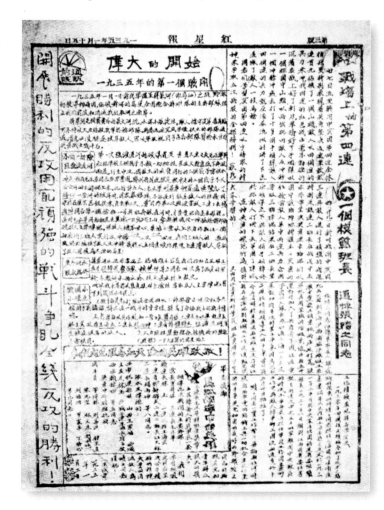

The Red Army never lost its social cohesion, even when on the run. Newspapers were printed as they traversed China. This edition tells of the capture of Luding Bridge. (Evergreen Pictures)

it was generally accepted by all that Nationalist forces were weakest there. In July 1935, the XXV Corps managed to break the news blackout, and for the first time (via an out-of-date newspaper) learned that Mao's First Red Army and Zhang's Fourth Red Army were both heading north in the general direction of Gansu and Shaanxi provinces. From then on, the aim was clear. Despite attrition due to sickness and combat, the XXV Corps still managed to grow in strength, and by the mid-summer of 1935, its combat strength had expanded to over 4,000 troops (the only force to witness an increase in manpower by the end of the Long March). Once again, cultural sensitivity when entering ethnic minority areas helped the Red recruitment cause.

On 16 September 1935, the XXV Corps met up with local Communists in the Shaanxi–Gansu–Ningxia Soviet (later renamed the Shaanxi–Gansu Border Area Soviet), who had been battling government troops for a number of years in an effort to keep hold of their base area. Xi Zhongxun, the father of the current President of China, Xi

Second Red Army and VI Corps' march

1. Red Army VI Corps led by Xiao Ke departs Jinggang Mountain on 7 August 1934.
2. Red Army VI Corps meets up with He Long's II Corps at Mu Huang on 24 October 1934.
3. Red Army VI and II Corps combine to form the Second Red Army, under He Long. They attempt to enlarge the size of the Hunan–Hebei–Jiangxi Soviet, with the arrival of Mao's First Red Army in mind.
4. In January 1935, the CCP decides that the First Red Army should not join up with the Second Red Army in Hunan. The Second Red Army embarks on its Long March to join up with the First Red Army in the Soviet in northern Shaanxi, commencing 19 November 1935.
5. Second Red Army joins up with Zhang Guotao's Fourth Red Army at Garzê on 30 June 1936. The XXXII Corps, formerly IX Corps of First Red Army, joins the Second Red Army.
6. Second Red Army ends its Long March in October 1936 in Jiangtaibao, just north of Jingning in Gansu Province, linking up with elements of First Red Army.

Communist insurgency zone
Soviet (in 1934/35)
HJS   Hunan–Jiangxi Soviet
HHJS   Hunan–Hubei–Jiangxi Soviet
SGNS   Shaanxi–Gansu–Ningxia Soviet
Proposed Soviet (not established)
New Soviet added 1936
Temporary Red Army concentration
Red Army VI Corps
Second Red Army
Nationalist troop concentration
Nationalist defensive line
Nationalist movements

0   200 miles
0   200km

80

Jinping, was the head of the Soviet, and received the XXV Corps on its arrival. Although it was the smallest of the four Red Army forces to take part in the Long March, the XXV Corps was the first to arrive in a safe haven in north-west China. The XXV Corps and the local Communists were able to remain there partly due to the inhospitable, highland desert terrain.

XXV Corps' Long March

Start date	16 November 1934
End date	15 September 1935
Distance	*c.* 4,500km
Manpower at start	2,987
Manpower at halfway point	1,300
Manpower at end	3,400

SECOND RED ARMY'S MARCH

The Second Red Army (as it later became known) began its withdrawal west from Hubei and embarked on its Long March only in November 1935, after Mao's First Red Army had reached its safe haven in northern Shaanxi. Its II Corps was led by He Long, a former rebel commander of the NRA's Twentieth Army, who in 1932 had established a Soviet in the border area between Hunan and Jiangxi (the Hunan–Jiangxi Soviet). As retribution for his disloyalty, Chiang Kaishek had He Long's three sisters and a brother executed.

Just before the Central (First) Red Army embarked on its Long March in October 1934, He Long's forces were strengthened by the arrival of the VI Corps from the Jinggang Mountains, commanded by Xiao Ke. He Long and Xiao Ke agreed a compromise between them, and the joint force of over 7,000 men (now known as the Second Red Army) would come under the command of He Long. The newly strengthened Red forces would go into battle almost immediately, launching a diversionary attack in western Hunan to draw Chiang's attention away from the escaping Central (First) Red Army and also to enlarge the Soviet. The success of He Long's attack alarmed the Nationalist leadership; at one point, the Second Red Army held the provincial capital Changsha as well as the two principal cities of Changde and Yueyang. The audacious actions by He Long worked, as Chiang recalled part of his army (the 16th, 19th and 62nd divisions) to deal with trouble caused.

In February 1935, Chiang diverted a further 80 regiments to attack He Long's forces in his expanded Soviet base (now known as the Hunan–Hubei–Sichuan–Guizhou Soviet). Under intense pressure following a series of defeats, the Second Red Army had to withdraw, and He's forces were reduced to 9,000 by March 1935. He Long's aggressive moves to expand the Soviet were partly driven by the orders given to him to rendezvous the Central (First) Red Army with the Second Red Army: to accommodate such a large force, He Long needed more space. However, after the Zunyi Conference in January 1935, the First Red Army decided not to meet up with the Second Red Army. The obvious question for He Long now was to decide whether his army should stay, or move to a new Soviet. Over the summer of 1935, despite being constantly under pressure, He Long successfully outmanoeuvred the Nationalist forces, inflicted over 10,000 enemy casualties and captured 8,000 prisoners of war. The Red Army used the latter to replenish its ranks, and He's army grew to 21,000. Alarmed by the increasingly audacious rebels, Chiang Kaishek increasd the number of NA troops deployed against He Long's army to 130 regiments. The vast majority of this force came from the elite, German-trained central army, loyal to Chiang. This plunged He Long into serious difficulties, and in early November 1935 the decision was taken to embark on their Long March to meet up with Zhang Guotao's Fourth Red Army; Zhang had telegraphed He Long 'instructing' him to obey him as the new Red Army commander.

On 19 November 1935, the Second Red Army set out, with three divisions (4th, 5th and 6th) under II Corps and another three divisions (16th, 17th and 18th) under VI Corps. Its 20,000 headed south towards Jing County, before turning west towards Qianxi in Guizhou Province. Learning from the mistakes of the First Red Army, its troops and followers travelled in light order, bearing three days of rations and up to six pairs of straw sandals each. The young and the old were to be left behind or given money to travel to other places. Once again, a stay-behind force (the 18th Division) remained to create a diversion and allow the main force to escape.

He Long's force was driven further west than the First Red Army, and by April 1936 had marched all the way to Lijiang in Yunnan Province. The Second Red Army then crossed the Jade Dragon Snow Mountain massif and headed through the highlands of western Sichuan. During the march, the

Huang Zhen was another artist who marched with the Red Army. Today, only 24 of his Long March sketches survive. After the foundation of the PRC, Huang ended up in the diplomatic corps and served as ambassador to Malaysia, the USA, Hungary and France. (Evergreen Pictures)

Second Red Army detained two European missionaries, Rudolf Bosshardt (who later wrote an account of his experiences) and Arnolis Hayman, for 16 months. On 30 June 1936, He Long met up with Zhang's Fourth Red Army at Garzê in Sichuan Province. The Second Red Army was subsequently strengthened by the addition of the XXXII Corps (formerly the IX Corps of the First Red Army), and eventually met up with the First Red Army at Jiangtaibao, near Jingning in Gansu Province, in October 1936, thus ending its Long March.

ABOVE LEFT
Mao shortly after the Long March. When he reached northern Shaanxi, he was 43 years old. Like many Long March veterans, he was suffering from malnourishment. (Evergreen Pictures)

ABOVE RIGHT
The rendezvous of the Second Red Army with the First Red Army in northern Shaanxi. Note the lack of support weapons in the Red Army in the mid-1930s. The only two rapid-fire weapons seen here are the two Czech-made ZB vz. 26 light machine guns, which remained the most common type in China until the end of World War II. These weapons had all been captured from the NA. (Bettmann via Getty Images)

Second Red Army's Long March

Start date	19 November 1935
End date	22 October 1936
Distance	c. 10,000km
Manpower at start	86,859 + 17,000 non-combatants
Manpower at halfway point	16,500
Manpower at end	13,300

VI Corps' Long March

Start date	August 1934
End date	24 October 1935
Distance	2,500km
Manpower at start	9,700
Manpower at end	3,300

AFTERMATH

After the great rendezvous of forces at the end of the Long March, the First, Second, Fourth and Fifteenth armies fought Chiang Kaishek's NA in the Battle of Mountain Fort between 20 and 22 November 1936. The Red forces destroyed most of the 232nd Brigade, thus ensuring the new Soviet in northern Shaanxi was secure.

In 1935 and 1936, while the CCP was busy defending its Soviets from Chiang's attacks, the propaganda department of the CCP focussed on a new message, calling for a ceasefire and labelling the Japanese as the real threat to China. In practical terms, the Reds were exhausted after the strains of the Long March. Chiang naturally did not wish to let this opportunity slip by and concentrated an even larger force against the Communists, who were now more or less all in one place. One of the reasons why Mao chose north-west China to end his Long March was that it was physically close to the Soviet Union, an important factor for the CCP, which still relied on Moscow for support. To maintain this lifeline, Zhang Guotao's Fourth Red Army took the lead in securing the north-west corridor for the CCP. However, poor decision-making during the crossing of the Yellow River saw many of Zhang's 21,800 remaining troops wiped out by more than 100,000 combined Muslim warlord troops under Ma Bufang, Ma Hongbin and Ma Zhongying.

This iconic pagoda in Yan'an became a symbol of the capital of the new CCP safe haven in north-west China. The CCP held on to Yan'an until it was abandoned in 1947. (Evergreen Pictures)

The principal leaders of the Red Army in Yan'an. From left to right: Bo Gu, Zhou Enlai, Zhu De and Mao Zedong. Bo Gu survived the purge in Zunyi, mainly because he was able to admit to and accept his mistakes, while Otto Braun and Zhang Guotao failed to do this. (Bettmann via Getty Images)

In December 1936, the 'Young Marshal' Zhang Xueliang held his leader Chiang Kaishek hostage in Xi'an, when the latter came to the capital of Shaanxi Province to admonish Zhang for not putting enough effort into his anti-communist campaign. For Zhang, the real enemies were the Japanese and not the CCP: it was the Japanese who forced him into exile from his beloved Manchuria, and the only force left in Manchuria to fight the Japanese comprised pro-Communist guerrillas. Despite receiving a promise from Chiang that Zhang's actions would not be punished, Chiang had Zhang

A bodyguard platoon protecting the CCP leadership stands to attention to receive visitors to Mao. This picture was almost certainly taken after 1937, when the Red Army had been incorporated into the Nationalist Army, evidenced by the white patch on top of the soldier's left breast pocket detailing the soldier's name, rank and unit. (Archiv Gerstenberg/ullstein bild via Getty Images)

A sentry post in Gansu. The post is camouflaged with branches to protect it from air attack. The two sentries are both armed with Mauser C96 semi-automatic pistols, a popular weapon in China since the early 1920s. (Evergreen Pictures)

arrested soon after he reached safety. Zhang's action cost him his freedom for the next 54 years. However, his action did pave the way for a formal ceasefire between the KMT and the CCP. After the Marco Polo Bridge Incident in July 1937 (where Chinese and Japanese troops clashed outside Beijing), the ceasefire was formalized, and a nominal alliance (the Second United Front) was formed between the two adversaries to fight the Japanese.

The Red Army was now heavily reorganized into two armies (Eighth Route Army and New Fourth Army) and nominally formed part of the NA's order of battle, but operationally it remained under CCP control. From 1937 to 1945, the two Communist-led armies fought a disciplined and well-organized guerrilla campaign against the Japanese. At the same time, they grew in size and matured into a potent fighting force. By the time the Japanese surrendered to the Communists in 1945, they were no longer 'bandits' – instead the newly renamed PLA fought like a regular field army. In 1949, the PLA succeeded in driving Chiang Kaishek and the KMT out of mainland China to the island of Taiwan.

CONCLUSION

The Long March was one of the most arduous and toughest odysseys in Chinese military history, and one of the longest retreats in the history of warfare. Of the over 86,000 troops of the Central (First) Red Army that embarked on the Long March, only around 33,000 survived. But from near destruction, it rose like a phoenix from the ashes. At the tiller of this transformation was Mao. The invincible spirit and will of the Red Army soldiers displayed in this journey help explain the final victory of the CCP. The near-constant combat and physical strain of the journey whittled out those not fully committed to the communist ideal, and the militarily incapable. What was left was a hardened, experienced, and extremely confident core. The final safe haven in the highlands of northern Shaanxi, where many of the Communists ended up living in caves, gave the CCP the protective isolation it needed, allowing its army to recuperate and rebuild. The new Soviet allowed the CCP to put its form of government into action, having learnt by trial and error how to garner the support of the peasants.

The Long March solidified Mao's status as the undisputed leader of the CCP. Other participants in the march also went on to become prominent leaders, including Zhu De (head of the PLA), Liu Shaoqi (president), Dong Biwu (vice president), Ye Jianying (head of state), Li Xiannian (president), Yang Shangkun (president), Zhou Enlai (prime minister and foreign minister) and Deng Xiaoping (the paramount leader of China from 1978 to the early 1990s). These were very tough individuals, both mentally and physically, and this served them well for

Communist-controlled areas after the Long March

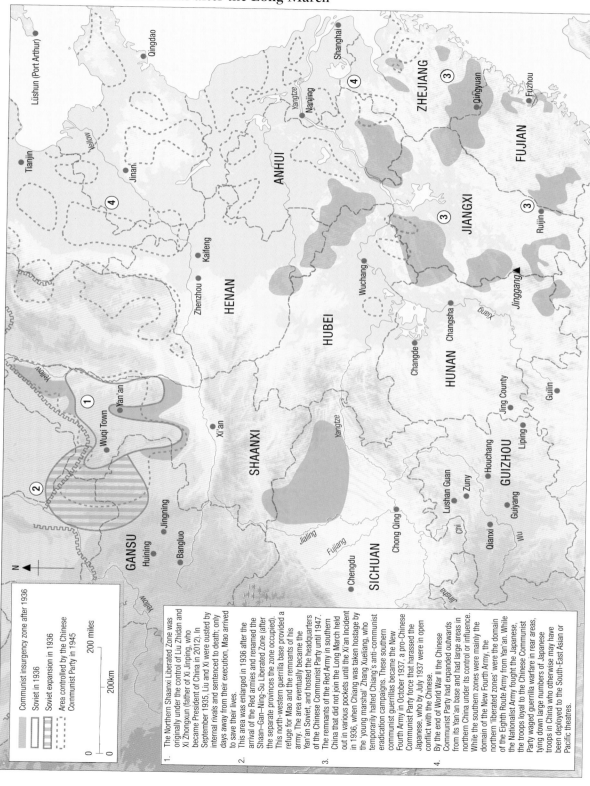

Lüshun (Port Arthur)

Qingdao

Tianjin

Jinan

Yellow

Qingdao

Shanghai

ZHEJIANG ④

③ Qingyuan

Fuzhou

FUJIAN ③

Yangtze

Nanjing

ANHUI

Kaifeng

HENAN

Zhenzhou

JIANGXI ③

Wuchang

③ Ruijin

Jinggang ▲

HUBEI

Guiang

Changde

HUNAN

Changsha

Yellow

Yan'an

④

① Wuqi Town

Xi'an

SHAANXI

Yangtze

Jing County

Guilin

②

Jingping

Bangluo

Huining

GANSU

Jialing

Fujiang

Chengdu

SICHUAN

Chong Qing

Jinsha

Chi

Lushan Guan

Zuny

Houchang

Qianxi

Wu

GUIZHOU

Liping

Guiyang

N ◀

Legend

Communist insurgency zone after 1936

Soviet in 1936

Soviet expansion in 1936

Area controlled by the Chinese Communist Party in 1945

0   200 miles
0   200km

1. The Northern Shaanxi Liberated Zone was originally under the control of Liu Zhidan and Xi Zhongxun (father of Xi Jinping, who became President of China in 2012). In September 1935, Liu and Xi were ousted by internal rivals and sentenced to death; only days away from their execution, Mao arrived to save their lives.

2. This area was enlarged in 1936 after the arrival of the Red armies and renamed the Shaan–Gan–Ning-Su Liberated Zone (after the separate provinces the zone occupied). This north-western guerrilla base provided a refuge for Mao and the remnants of his army. The area eventually became the Yan'an Soviet, and hosted the headquarters of the Chinese Communist Party until 1947.

3. The remnants of the Red Army in southern China that did not join the Long March held out in various pockets until the Xi'an Incident in 1936, when Chiang was taken hostage by the 'young marshal' Zhang Xueliang, who temporarily halted Chiang's anti-communist eradication campaigns. These southern communist guerrillas became the New Fourth Army in October 1937, a pro-Chinese Communist Party force that harassed the Japanese, who by July 1937 were in open conflict with the Chinese.

4. By the end of World War II the Chinese Communist Party had expanded outwards from its Yan'an base and had large areas in northern China under its control or influence. While the southern zones were mainly the domain of the New Fourth Army, the northern 'liberated zones' were the domain of the Eighth Route Army from Yan'an. While the troops loyal to the Chinese Communist Party waged guerrilla warfare in rear areas, tying down large numbers of Japanese troops in China who otherwise may have been deployed to the South-East Asian or Pacific theatres.

many years after the foundation of the PRC on 1 October 1949. Indeed, some historians have suggested that the reason the PRC outsurvived the USSR was because many of the Long March veterans were still active in politics in the PRC up to the early 1990s. The greatest loser of the Long March was Zhang Guotao, who was purged in 1937 from the CCP, and defected to the KMT in 1938. Instead of being welcomed with great celebrations, Zhang was sidelined, holding only minor posts while devoid of any power, resources or support. In 1949, he chose to go into exile in Hong Kong, and 20 years later emigrated to Canada to join his two sons, who were already living in Toronto. He died in a nursing home on 3 December 1979 at the age of 82.

How did a ragtag army equipped with hand-me-down weapons defeat a superior regular army backed by artillery and air power? One reason is Chiang Kaishek's style of leadership: he constantly interfered with his field commanders' decisions, creating unnecessary confusion. He would bypass the formal command structure, and from his HQ hundreds of kilometres away from the fighting, would call a front-line battalion commander and instruct him on how to deploy his troops. Regimental commanders would suddenly find that their battalions had been moved to another location without any notification, throwing any battle plans into total disarray. According to Yan Daogang, a former chief of staff to Chiang: 'After [Chiang] heard that the Red Army had crossed the Wu River [on 31 March 1935], he went into a fit of rage and took direct control of the army, bypassing the decision-making process, rendering General Xue Yue nothing more than a high-level messenger.' A second reason was the way in which the NA operated. In June 1947, in the midst of the civil war, in a speech to senior commanders of his army Chiang identified the heart of the problem: 'The National Army does not attach importance to the participation of soldiers.' The opinions of low-level commanders and soldiers were routinely ignored, in contrast to the 'democratic' approach of the Communists in their battle planning. Indeed, the Red Army's *Combat Handbook* clearly stated: 'Of fundamental importance to winning battles is high troop moral ... Rally the troops, encourage every soldier to do his best, encourage everyone to speak out and support each other.'

A typical home in Yan'an. Many people in northern Shaanxi lived in caves like this, including Mao and his wife, as well as all of the leaders of the CCP during their time there. (Granger, NYC/TopFoto)

THE BATTLEFIELD TODAY

The areas through which the Long March passed remain inaccessible. However, for the determined few, there are several key sites that can be visited thanks to modern transport. The Jinggang Mountains, where Mao had his first Soviet, are today a key destination for tourists interested in China's revolutionary past. Visitors to the area can see the Red Army mint, the Revolution Museum and the Martyrs' Cemetery. The site is served by a local airport. Another key destination is the capital for Mao's Soviet, Ruijin, the setting-off point for Mao and his Central (First) Red Army on the Long March. Ruijin is located in Jiangxi Province, and in central Ruijin there is a museum. The easiest way to get to Ruijin is by train, a ten-hour journey from Shanghai.

Luding Bridge, another key site, is located in Luding County in Garzê Tibetan Autonomous Prefecture in Sichuan Province. Luding Bridge can only be reached by bus or taxi, and the easiest way is to set off from Ya'an City some 80km away. This area was at the epicentre of a very large earthquake in 2008, but has since been rebuilt. There is a modest toll charge to cross the bridge.

Zunyi, where the historic conference occurred, is located in Guizhou Province and can be reached easily by aeroplane. From Shanghai, it is a three-

Luding Bridge is today one of the top tourist destinations in China. Young people, many from state institutions, are offered subsidized holidays to places where Chinese communist history was made. Many get into the mood by dressing like the Red Army. (Zbigniew Bzdak/Chicago Tribune/MCT via Getty Images)

Behind this row of terraced houses in Shanghai lies the birthplace of the CCP. Between 21 and 31 July 1921, 13 men gathered here to hammer out the first constitution of the CCP in what was to be the first party congress. Three-quarters of the way through the meeting, the group was visited by the police and had to relocate to a tourist boat on South Lake in Jiaxing, Zhejiang Province, to finish the meeting. This site is now a museum, easily reached by metro, and entry is free. (Author's collection)

hour flight or by high-speed train a ten-hour ride. The building where the meeting was held is now a museum.

One further accessible site from the Long March is Yan'an, the endpoint of the march, and the centre of the Chinese communist revolution from 1936 to 1948. Yan'an is well served by express roads, high-speed trains and has its own airport. In Yan'an, no place is more sacred than Zaoyuan, a former orchard where Mao and his colleagues lived in caves carved out of the mountainside. The Yan'an Revolutionary Museum has a range of artefacts on display, including Mao's pistol and his taxidermied white pony.

The site of the foundation meeting of the CCP is located in Shanghai in Xintiandi, a popular tourist destination in the heart of the city. It is easily accessible by taxi and underground. Shanghai also hosted the second and fourth CCP congresses, the sites of which are also located in the heart of Shanghai and easily accessible by public transport. All these sites can be accessed free of charge.

On the other side of the world, in Pine Hills Cemetery in east Toronto, Canada, lies the grave of Zhang Guotao. His simple, unadorned tombstone tucked between two shrubs in section 5, plot 2263 marks the resting place of a man who could have changed history.

After the 1937 Marco Polo Bridge Incident, a truce was declared between the Communists and the Nationalist, and the Red Army was incorporated into the Nationalist Army. Seen here are members of the Eighth Route Army sometime in 1938, after China had begun to receive US aid, as evidenced by the Thompson machine guns the soldiers are carrying. (From the American Geographical Society Library, University of Wisconsin-Milwaukee Libraries)

APPENDIX

LIST OF CHINESE NAMES

Ai Zhong Xin (艾中信, 1915–2003)

Bai Chongxi (白崇禧, 1890–1966)

Bo Gu (博古, a.k.a. Qin Bangxian 秦邦宪, 1907–46)

Cai Shufan (蔡树藩,1905–58)

Cai Shun (蔡畅, 1900–90)

Chai E (蔡锷, 1882–1916)

Chen Changho (陈昌浩, 1906–67)

Chen Cheng (陈诚, 1897–1965)

Chen Congying (陈琼英,1902–2003)

Chen Duxiu (陈独秀, 1879–1942)

Chen Geng (陈赓, 1903–61)

Chen Guang (陈光, 1905–54)

Chen Jicheng (陈继承, 1893–1971)

Chen Jiongming (陈炯明, 1878–1933)

Chen Jitang (陈济棠, 1890–1954)

Cheng Sicai (程世才, 1912–1990)

Cheng Zihua (程子华, 1905–91)

Chiang Kaishek (蒋介石, 1887–1975)

Deng Xiaoping (邓小平, 1904–97)

Dong Biwu (董必武, 1886–1975)

Dong Zhentang (董振堂, 1895–1937)

Fan Songpu (樊崧甫, 1894–1979)

Feng Yuxiang (冯玉祥, 1882–1948)

Gao Gang (高岗, 1905–54)

Gu Zhutong (顾祝同, 1893–1987)

He Jian (何键, 1887–1956)

He Long (贺龙, 1896–1969)

He Wei (何畏, 1900–60)

He Zizhen (贺子珍, 1910–84)

Hu Zongnan (胡宗南, 1896–1962)

Huang Su (黄甦, 1908–35)

Huang Zhen (黄镇, 1909–89)

Jiang Dingwen (蒋鼎文, 1893–1974)

Le Shaohua (乐少华, 1903–52)

Li Dazhao (李大钊, 1888–1927)

Li Xiannian (李先念, 1909–92)

Li Yangjing (李扬敬, 1894–1988)

Li Yannian (李延年, 1904–74)

Li Zhuoran (李卓然, 1899–1989)

Liao Chengzhi (廖承志, 1908–83)

Lin Biao (林彪, 1907–71)

Lin Yuying (林育英, 1897–1942)

Liu Bocheng (刘伯承, 1892–1986)

Liu Heding (刘和鼎, 1894–1969)

Liu Jianchu (刘建緒, 1890–1978)

Liu Shaoqi (刘少奇, 1898–1969)

Liu Wenhui (刘文辉, 1895–1976)

Liu Yalou (刘亚楼, 1910–65)

Liu Ying (刘英, 1905–42)

Liu Yingu (刘膺古, 1895/7?–1966)

Liu Xiang (刘湘, 1890–1938)

Liu Xing (刘兴, 1887–1963)

Liu Zhidan (刘志丹, 1903–36)

Long Yun (龙云, 1884–1962)

Luo Binghui (罗炳辉, 1897–1946)

Luo Ruiqing (罗瑞卿, 1906–78)

Luo Zhuoying (罗卓英, 1896–1961)

Ma Bufang (马步芳, 1903–75)

Ma Hongbin (马鸿宾, 1884–1960)

Ma Zhongying (马仲英, 1910–36)

Mao Bingwen (毛炳文, 1891–1970)

Mao Zedong (毛泽东, 1893–1976)

Mao Zetang (毛泽覃, 1905–35)

Nie Rongzheng (聂荣臻, 1899–1992)

Pan Hannian (潘汉年, 1906–77)

Pang Bingxun (庞炳勋, 1879–1963)

Peng Dehuai (彭德怀, 1898–1974)

Puyi (溥仪, 1906–67)

Qian Dajun (钱大钧, 1893–1982)

Ren Bishi (任弼时, 1904–50)

Sheng Shicai (盛世才, 1897–1970)

Sun Chuanfang (孙传芳, 1885–1935)

Sun Du (孙渡, 1898–1967)

Sun Yatsen (孙逸仙, 1866–1925)

Tang Enbo (汤恩伯, 1898–1954)

Wang Hongkun (王宏坤, 1909–93)

Wang Jialie (王家烈, 1893–1966)

Wang Jiaxiang (王稼祥, 1906–74)

Wang Jingjiu (王敬久, 1902–64)

Wang Kaixiang (王开湘, 1908–35)

Wang Ming (王明, 1904–74)

Wang Ruci (王如痴, 1903–35)

Wang Shoudao (王首道, 1906–96)

Wang Shusheng (王树声, 1905–74)

Wang Weizhou (王维舟,1887–1970)

Wang Zhen (王震, 1908–93)

Wei Lihuang (卫立煌 1897-1960)

Wu Chengren (伍诚仁, 1896–1970)

Wu Huanxian (吴焕先, 1907–35)

Wu Qiwei (吴奇伟, 1891–1953)
Xi Jinping (习近平, 1953–)
Xi Zhongxun (习仲勋, 1913–2002)
Xia Ming (夏明, dates unknown)
Xiang Hanping (香翰屏, 1890–1978)
Xiang Ying (项英, 1895?–1941)
Xiao Ke (萧克, 1907–2008)
Xu Donghai (徐东海, 1900–70)
Xu Haidong (徐海东, 1900–70)
Xu Shiyou (许世友, 1905–85)
Xu Xiangqian (徐向前, 1901–90)
Xue Yue (薛岳, 1896–1998)
Xun Zhunzhou (寻淮洲, 1912–34)
Yan Daogang (晏道刚, 1889–1973)
Yang Cheng-wu (杨成武, 1914–2004)
Yang Dezhi (杨得志, 1911–94)
Yang Hucheng (杨虎城, 1893–1949)
Yang Kaihui (杨开慧, 1901–30)
Yang Keming (杨克明, 1905–37)

Yang Shangkun (杨尚昆, 1907–98)
Ye Jianying (叶剑英, 1897–1986)
Yu Hanmou (余汉谋, 1896–1981)
Yu Tianyun (余天云, 1906–36)
Yu Xuezhong (于学忠, 1890–1964)
Yuan Shikai (袁世凯, 1859–1916)
Zeng Guofan (曾国藩, 1811–72)
Zhan Caifang (詹才芳, 1907–92)
Zhang Guangcai (张广才, 1900–70)
Zhang Guotao (张国焘, 1897–1979)
Zhang Wentian (张闻天, 1900–76)
Zhang Xueliang (张学良, 1901–2001)
Zhang Zuolin (张作霖, 1875–1928)
Zhou Chunquan (周纯全, 1905–85)
Zhou Enlai (周恩来, 1898–1976)
Zhou Hunyuan (周浑元, 1895–1938)
Zhou Kun (周昆, 1902–?)
Zhu De (朱德, 1886–1976)

LIST OF CHINESE PLACE NAMES

Abe (啊坝)
Baizhang Pass (百丈关)
Bangluo Town (榜罗镇)
Banyou (班佑)
Baxi (巴西)
Changban Mountain (长板山)
Changde (常德)
Changde Mountain (仓德山)
Changsha (长沙)
Chengdu (成都)
Chi (Red) River (赤水河)
Dabie Mountain (大别山)
Dadu River (大渡河)
Dagu Mountain (打古山)
Danba (丹巴)
Dushu Village (Lone Tree Town, 独树镇)
Ejie (俄界)
Fujian (福建)
Fujiang (涪江)
Funiu Mountain (伏牛山)
Ganquan (甘泉)
Garzê (甘孜)
Guiyang (贵阳)
Gutian (古田)
Hubei (湖北)
Huining (会宁)
Hunan (湖南)
Jade Dragon Snow Mountain (玉龙雪山)

Jiajin Mountain (夹金山)
Jialing River (嘉陵江)
Jiangtaibao (将台堡)
Jiangxi (江西)
Jiaoping Crossing (皎平渡口)
Jing County (靖县)
Jinggang Mountains (井冈山)
Jingning (静宁)
Jinsha River (金沙江)
Jiaxing (嘉兴)
Kunming (昆明)
Kyom Kyo (Zhuomudiao 卓木调/Jiaomuzu 脚木足)
Lianghekou (两河口)
Lijiang (丽江)
Liping (黎平)
Longjie Crossing (龙街渡口)
Luding Bridge (泸定桥)
Lugquan (禄劝)
Lushan (芦山)
Lushan Guan (娄山关)
Mao'ergai (毛儿盖)
Maogong (懋功/Xiaojin County 小金县)
Mengbi Mountain (梦笔山)
Mu Huang (木黄)
Qianxi (黔西)
Ruijin (瑞金)
Shaguo (沙锅)
Shangrao (上饶)

Shawo (砂窝)
Tongbo Mountain (桐柏山)
Tongdao (通道)
Wayaobao (瓦窑堡)
Wu River (乌江)
Wuchang (武昌)
Wuding (武定)
Ya'an City (雅安)

Yuanmao (元谋)
Yudu River (雩都河/Gong Water 贡水)
Yueyang (岳阳)
Zaoyang County (枣阳县)
Zhaxi (扎西)
Zhejiang (浙江)
Zhongxi (重溪)
Zunyi (遵义)

ABBREVIATIONS AND GLOSSARY

CCP — Chinese Communist Party.

COMINTERN — Communist International, officially known as the 'Third Socialist International'. Its purpose was to coordinate between the Communist Party of the Soviet Union and revolutionary groups in other countries. Disbanded in 1949.

KMT — Kuomintang, the Chinese Nationalist Party.

NA — National Army – the post-1928 name of the National Revolutionary Army.

NRA — National Revolutionary Army – formed from the KMT and CCP in 1923 to end warlordism in China.

PLA — People's Liberation Army, the armed forces of the CCP after 1945.

PRC — People's Republic of China – established in 1949 after the Chinese Civil War resulted in a division of territory between mainland China and the island of Taiwan.

ROC — Republic of China – the official Chinese national state name between 1912 and 1949.

Soviet — An autonomous Communist base area, which contained a complete political, administrative and military infrastructure.

The Red Army colours, in Yan'an sometime in the late 1930s. Note the poor quality of the soldier's uniform and his youthfulness. (From the American Geographical Society Library, University of Wisconsin-Milwaukee Libraries)

In 1955, the ten former field commanders of the PLA were promoted to the prestigious rank of marshal. Shown here is Zhu De, who was one of the ten. The only one of the ten who was not a veteran of the Long March was Chen Yi. (Author's collection)

The original first edition of Edgar Snow's book *Red Star Over China*. The friendship between Snow and Mao began after the American made the journey to Yan'an to meet the Communist leader, despite attempts by the Nationalists to prevent him from doing so. Snow and Mao struck up a lifelong friendship, and after meeting Snow, Mao's fame spread beyond China to the rest of the world. (Author's collection)

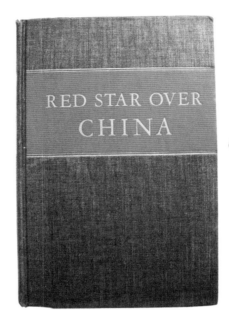

BIBLIOGRAPHY

Bosshardt, R. A., *The Restraining Hand: Captivity for Christ in China*, Hodder & Stoughton: London, 1936

Chinese Historical Documents, Vol. III: *Yan Daogang (Chiang Kaishek's Anti-Bandit Campaign during the Long March: Deployments and Defeat)*, Chinese Literature and History Press: Beijing, 1996 (in Chinese)

Hayman, Arnolis (ed. Brady, Anne-Marie), *A Foreign Missionary on the Long March: The Memoirs of Arnolis Hayman of the China Inland Mission*, MerwinAsia: Portland, ME, 2010

Frtiz, Jean, *China's Long March: 6,000 Miles of Danger*, Putnam Juvenile: New York, 1988

McEwen, Andrew J., *The Long March: The True Story Behind the Legendary Journey that Made Mao's China*, Constable & Robinson Ltd: London, 2006

Snow, Edgar, *Red Star Over China*, Penguin Books: Harmondsworth, 1972. First published in 1937, this is undoubtedly the best book, and the first book in English, to tell the story of the Long March. Many editions are available, in several languages.

Life magazine (25 January 1937): 'First Pictures of China's Roving Communists', pp. 9–14

Salisbury, Charlotte Y., *Long March Diary: China Epic*, Walker & Co: New York, 1986

Salisbury, Harrison E., *The Long March: The Untold Story*, McGaw-Hill, New York, 1987

Sun Shuyun, *The Long March*, Harper Perennial: London, 2007

Wilson, Dick, *The Long March 1935: The Epic of Chinese Communism's Survival*, Viking: New York, 1971

Zhang Guotao, *My Memories*, 3 volumes, Oriental Press: Beijing, 1998 (in Chinese)

Snow's *Red Star Over China* is known as *The 25,000-Li Westward March* in China – a *li* being a Chinese mile, equivalent to *c.* 500m. (Author's collection)

INDEX

Page numbers in **bold** refer to illustrations.